MIND OVER MATTER

Also by Jordin Tootoo with Stephen Brunt

All the Way: My Life on Ice

JORDIN TOOTOO

with STEPHEN BRUNT

HARD-WON BATTLES on the ROAD to HOPE

MIND OVER MATTER

VIKING

VIKING
an imprint of Penguin Canada,
a division of Penguin Random House Canada Limited

Canada • USA • UK • Ireland • Australia •
New Zealand • India • South Africa • China

First published 2022

www.penguinrandomhouse.ca

LIBRARY AND ARCHIVES CANADA CATALOGUING IN PUBLICATION

Title: Mind over matter : hard-won battles on the road to hope/
Jordin Tootoo with Stephen Brunt.
Names: Tootoo, Jordin, 1983- author. | Brunt, Stephen, author.
Identifiers: Canadiana (print) 20210395265 | Canadiana (ebook) 20210395273 |
ISBN 9780735242265 (hardcover) | ISBN 9780735242272 (EPUB)
Subjects: LCSH: Tootoo, Jordin, 1983- | LCSH: Inuit hockey players—Biography. |
LCSH: Hockey players—Canada—Biography. | LCSH: Fathers and sons.
| LCGFT: Autobiographies.
Classification: LCC GV848.5.T66 A3 2022 | DDC 796.962092—dc23

Book design by Lisa Jager
Cover design by Lisa Jager
Cover image by Pete Thompson

Printed in the United States of America

10 9 8 7 6 5 4 3 2 1

This book is dedicated to my parents, Rose and Barney. Life wasn't always easy, but I love you more today than I ever have. I owe my life to you.

To forgive is not just to be altruistic. It is the best form of self-interest. . . . If you can find it in yourself to forgive, then you are no longer chained to the perpetrator.
—Desmond Tutu, *The Book of Forgiving: The Fourfold Path for Healing Ourselves and Our World*

Contents

1 We Are Still Connected

In June 2021, I went on a fishing trip with my advisor and close friend, Mike Watson. We were in the middle of the COVID-19 pandemic, and it was one of the few times I had been away from our home in more than a year. I thought it would be a way for me to rejuvenate the soul, revitalize my energy and spirit.

"Hon, I'm going to come back a changed man," I said to my wife, Jennifer, the day before I left. "It's time to go."

I drove up from my house in Kelowna on a Friday evening, stayed at Watty's place in Vancouver, and then we got up early Saturday morning and took the ferry to Nanaimo on Vancouver Island before heading north. I was driving and Watty was riding in the passenger seat. That's when I got that fucking text from my sister, Corinne.

Every time I get a text from family, the first thing I think is "Fuck. What now?"

"Hey Jordin," it said. "Hope you're doing well. I hate to ask this, but can you send me money? I want to play bingo tonight."

Here we go again. What fucking fake story do I have to give now to get out of this? Jen is always telling me to just be honest with them, just tell them no. But I feel the guilt. What kind of excuse can I use?

Corinne knew I was going on a fishing trip, and I think her tactic was to try and get me just before I went off the grid.

I sat there, silently. I was internalizing it. I was irate. Mike knows better than to say anything to me when I'm like that. After about twenty minutes, I handed him my phone and showed him the message from my sister. We talked about it a little bit. There was more silence.

Then I started talking about my father, Barney Tootoo.

The connection I was making isn't easy to explain. It wasn't directly because of the text. My dad was never the one to ask for financial help. Any time I asked him, "Hey Dad, what do you need?" he'd say, "Nothing." If he did accept money, it was always for fuel and ammunition. I knew that it was going to be put to proper use.

I think what triggered my thoughts was the fact that we were going out "on the land," the way we do at home in Nunavut. I was putting my feet in my dad's boots. On the land is where he's at peace. Out there, money doesn't matter. You're on your own. Whatever you do in those moments is all that matters—living in the now.

Over the last few years, I have been trying to navigate in my head how to approach my dad about questions I have about his life. That weighs heavy on me in those quiet moments. Why can't it just be simple?

When I was a kid, both of our parents instilled fear in us, but my dad way more than my mom, Rose. A lot of his emotional, violent breakouts happened when he was under the influence of alcohol. There'd be tension in the house while everyone was waiting for my dad to get out on the land to escape reality. Dad demands respect to feel love. If you don't put food on the table and do acts of service for him, he'll turn the tables on you when he's half-cut. My mom knows that storyline all too well, and when Dad is about to go off, she gets out of Dodge.

After a weekend bender, it was almost like clockwork. He would know he'd done something stupid or been verbally abusive the night before. The next day, he'd sit up in his room for hours in the morning, and then he'd finally come down and leave the house to go for fresh air. He obviously didn't want to be seen because he knew damn well he had been a fucking asshole the night before. He'd head out to the cabin and escape everything that happened. Let everything cool down while he was away.

Growing up, that's how it was. My dad would party, and the next day he'd go out on the land for a day or two until everything settled down. Then he'd come home with food from the hunt.

A lot of times when we were young, my brother, Terence, and I would go with him. Even though Dad was hung to the gills, he was still on point when he was out on the land. I think of it now as being like I was when I played "guilty hockey" back in my drinking days. Partying the night before and then playing the next day, trying to show no weakness. I feel like I learned that from my dad. He would still reek of booze, but as soon as we got out of town, he was in a different mental state.

When we were together out on the land, I'd look over at Dad and see him sitting there, staring off in the distance. What was he thinking about? I wanted to shout, "What's going through your head, Dad?" I replay those moments all the time. But if I actually asked that question, I feel like he would give me an answer like, "Oh, I'm just looking for caribou." He would never be honest about what was really going on in his mind, because he didn't want to show weakness—that manly pride, right?

When I see my dad in silence now, I wonder if he is reminiscing about times he had with Terence. I know the pain he's going through because of the loss of my brother. But he'll never show it.

That's what I was silently thinking about in the car that day after my sister sent the text. And then I said it out loud.

"Why does he behave that way?"

In October 2019, right before I announced my retirement from the NHL, I wrote a letter to my dad. It was part of the therapy that I have continued since going to rehab and getting sober in 2010.

This is what it said:

Hey Dad, I'm just in Kelowna and thought I'd send you a quick note. Today's a little rainy and windy in the Okanagan Valley. It was so nice to have you here for my retirement party and to see you chat with a bunch of my hockey buddies. I'm hoping it brought back some amazing memories we had throughout my hockey career. I'm sure you probably miss coming south to watch me play and enjoy the nightlife in Nashville. What a great city that was. I'm thinking it was your favourite city, eh? Anyways, I was just thinking about a few things after you left Kelowna. My mind was racing with a ton of questions I have for you regarding your life.

As we all know, my childhood was dysfunctional. And there was a lot of chaos in our household. But at the same time, we have had many great memories together out on the land. Not so much when we were at home on the weekends. Every time we are out on the land, I want to ask some hard questions. But I was always afraid to ask because I didn't want to ruin the moment while we were out hunting or fishing. I often reflect on life when we are out on the land. I know that Terence was your right-hand man. He was the one that looked after you and helped you. While growing up, I would ask myself, "Why do you treat him like shit when you are drunk and when you are sober you treat him with love and kindness?"

When I look back, you honestly were Dr. Jekyll and

Mr. Hyde. Amazing person when you are sober, but a train wreck when you are drunk. The question I have for you is: Why are you the way you are when you are drunk? Did something happen to you as a kid? Is there something deeper that is making you drink as much as you do? The anger I see from you is painful to see when you are drunk. As adults, I just want to know what really happened. The time you told me I wasn't your son really made me angry with you. Do you remember that? I think it's time for us to try and get past the anger, the hurt, the shame or whatever it may be. I just want you to be open and honest and tell me the whole story.

I won't judge, I will always love you no matter what. The emotional abuse needs to stop. The constant yelling and demanding respect has to stop. I hate watching you beat down on Mom emotionally.

Today's a new day for all of us. And I just want to write you a quick note because I needed to get it off my back. I have my own family and I've changed my life cycle so the cycle doesn't continue. I have forgiven you because I needed to for my own health. The cycle stops with me. I will forever love you no matter what, Dad. I'm looking forward to our next trip out on the land and hoping you will start to talk about your life. It's time for us to move forward and let go of the anger, pain, hurt and shame.

Hope this finds you well today. Until we meet again, Dad, love you.

I wrote a letter to my mom a couple of days later:

Dear Mom, I'm hoping this finds you well. I'm here in Kelowna with Jen and the little ones enjoying the beautiful weather. One of the many reasons why we chose to call this home. The girls are sure growing up fast. And like you've always told me, time sure flies by. Siena had school today. And Avery ran errands all day with Jen.

Today I'm reminiscing about all the great qualities you instilled in me as a young kid. Here are just a couple. Respect, hard worker, giving. The fact that you always protected us from the many nightmare nights we had when Dad was drinking. Although I'm very grateful for these qualities, the truth is, I was always a fragile kid who was brutally scared to walk into our home.

Looking back, I'm very disappointed how our home was not a safe place for me to just be a kid. The constant yelling, screaming, fighting, amongst our family was very frightening for me. As time passed, the buildup of anger and resentment towards you and Dad grew immensely. And we all know what happened the summer when I beat the shit out of Dad. Yes, I was at my wit's end with the constant verbal and physical abuse from you and Dad. It was time for me to step up and defend myself. Your constant yelling had consumed me. And today I get to finally let go of it. I will not be talked down to anymore. I will not accept verbal manipulation from you or anyone else.

Trust me, I love you from the bottom of my heart. But it's time for me to move forward and let go of the anger, pain, guilt and resentment. Please know, in order for us to have a better relationship, we both need to ask for professional help. I'm doing my part in learning how to better myself for my family, and to have a better relationship with you. The constant "playing the victim" role, the "poor me" attitude needs to stop. Let's be real here. Stop hiding behind closed doors. It does us no good. Yes, I do wish we had a safe household as a kid and more love and affection towards each other as a kid. I've changed my life to stop one cycle and start a new cycle for my family.

I'm very grateful for everything that I've experienced in my life. And now I have the opportunity to look at life from a different perspective.

In closing, I want you to know that I always loved my mother no matter what. I will do the best I can to help you and tell you I love you every day. Although we may not talk every day. Just know I'm always thinking about you and the family.

Love you, Mom.

I never hit "send" on either one of those.

When I was writing them, I was releasing the weight from my shoulders. I thought, "This is making me feel good and I'll send them soon. No problem."

Then I'd talk to my mom and she'd be in a happy mood and I'd think, "I can't send her this." I was looking for excuses not to.

But with my dad, it's that fucking hurdle. That little fucking monkey on my back. I over-analyze this shit too much instead of just fucking doing it. This procrastination that I have about these tough questions is my own battle. I've got to confront it, like I've done with everything else in my life. It's very complicated. If I were to talk to one of my buddies about it, they would never understand, because it would take days to explain why I am the way I am today. And the last thing I want to do is start getting into the reasons why I'm scared, or the reasons why these walls fucking come up. Writing my first book helped me heal through certain parts of my life—mainly my sobriety, and how to stay on track. But there's way deeper shit.

In the car with Mike, I started asking more questions out loud about my father. Does he feel guilty? Does he feel shame? Fuck, what's going through his head? Why is he so silent?

But as soon as we got to our fishing cabin, I knew nothing could bother me there. I was on the land. I felt relieved because we were in familiar territory for me, away from society. I felt a sense of release. I was in a place where no one wanted nothing from me.

Mike's wife's cousin Michael and his son Cameron were already there. Cameron is a varsity lacrosse player down in the States. Talking to him, I knew I was with someone who understood the life of an athlete. We told similar stories. The one thing I really miss since I retired from hockey is being around the guys and that brotherhood that we shared. I felt an instant connection with Cameron. And then I watched father and son working together. Michael would tell his son to do these random chores and no questions asked, he just did it. It reminded me of my younger days and my dad telling me to walk down to the sled and grab the shovel or some other little, small task. A father telling his son to do something and allowing him to make the right choice—and if it wasn't the right one, my dad was never one to say you did it wrong. He would just analyze and silently re-tie the quad or whatever the job was.

But that was only when we were out on the land. When we got home and something needed to be done around the house, he'd be shouting, "Get the fucking thing done right now." It was a totally different dynamic.

Michael and Cameron went home the next day. Our guide arrived and gave me a couple of pointers, and again it brought back more memories of when I was a kid up in Nunavut. The guide was probably the same age as me, or younger, but he taught me the way my dad taught me out on the land: it's okay if it doesn't work out or if it's not right; we'll fix it, we'll get it right. It was the gentle way he explained things, tying on the nymphs and other little pointers.

I went and did what he said and I was just hammering the fish. And I was thinking what a fucking beautiful day this was. I wished my brother were here right now. Just being in silence, like when we were kids out on Big Meliadine Lake, bringing in the trout. Visualizing all those moments I had alone with my brother. That's where I feel his presence the most: when I'm out there with the rivers flowing.

I was kind of in a daydream. It was like Terence was right there with me—me and my bro, out fishing. I caught myself looking to my side, and then thinking, "Oh, fuck, he's not there." But it brought joy to me knowing that I'm able to share these moments, spiritually, with him. Showing him that I'm still here, and that we are still connected.

2 What Did He Experience?

By the time we got off the river the next day, we had fished for something like thirty hours. We were physically exhausted but felt great. We drove into Campbell River and went into the local Boston Pizza for dinner.

The story about the discovery of the graves outside the old Kamloops Indian Residential School had come out just a day or two before we went fishing. I had read a little bit about it before I left home. But that night, Mike called up a story on his phone and handed it to me. In the article, one of the residential school survivors was talking about what it was like. He said, "If we looked up at them, they would beat us. If we spoke in our native tongue, they would wash our mouths out with soap. If we misbehaved, they would wash our skin with lye, to change the colour because we are dirty."

On one of the nights we were at the fishing cabin, while we

were cooking dinner, I had a conversation with Watty about religion and the Catholic church. My wife, Jen, is from an Italian family and was raised Catholic. She wants to raise our kids in the church. But being in a church is not my thing, and I'm not going to be forced into something that doesn't interest me. My thing is spirituality, out on the land. That's what I'm going to show my kids.

I don't really know anything about organized religion. Jen knows my family history and how we're not religious, but she still wants our kids to grow up in the church. I knew Watty was raised a Catholic, so I talked to him about that, and about what I thought was the difference between religion and spirituality—the kind of spirituality I experienced when I felt my brother's presence out fishing that day.

But now I was thinking about the church in a whole other way. I felt anger, rage. My guts were turning. How could those priests and nuns fucking treat those kids the way that they did?

There was an older lady sitting a couple booths in front of us that night—a Native lady. A Stanley Cup playoff game was playing on the TV. I was reading the story, and as I looked up, this lady was cheering because Montreal had just scored and she was obviously a big Montreal fan. I looked at her, and instantly I could see my father.

My mind was racing, replaying all those moments where my dad was raging. And I was thinking about those kids in the residential schools and wondering, "Fuck, did that shit happen to him?" This is a big possibility. I could be wrong, but I just felt like I could connect it with my dad's behaviour when he's pissed drunk.

"What are you thinking about?" Mike asked me.

"My dad," I said. "This explains everything."

But of course I didn't really know. Maybe something else happened to him. I don't know because I don't know his fucking story. Reading this, you may be saying, "But how could you not know your father's story?" As a son, you'd think I would know everything about my parents. But the truth is, I don't—because nobody talked. Nobody ever fucking talked. My dad and me, we've never had heart-to-heart conversations about his life. He's just never been that guy. Even talking with other people in the family, everything's been hush-hush.

Where exactly did you grow up? Where did you move to? Little random things you'd think your family would talk about openly. Where did you guys travel? What were your experiences like? Nothing.

This is everything I know about my father's life: I know he was born and raised out on the land, living as a nomad. Because of a book that was written about the old ways of life called *Where the Foxes Roam*, I know that his mother had two husbands—an Inuk husband and a white husband. They were both hunters. That's why I have aunts and uncles and cousins with both the Tootoo and Hicks last names. I know that at some point my dad's family moved off the land and settled in Churchill, Manitoba, but I don't know why they did that when they did.

I often wonder why the Tootoo and Hicks family ended up in Churchill, but I assume it was because it was the closest big city to Nunavut. Back in the sixties and seventies there were seven thousand people living there. Now there are only five hundred. It was a big port with a big military presence, so that's where everyone congregated, because that's where the work was. And that's where the substance abuse started. They came in off the land and everything was at their fingertips.

What made them move to Whale Cove, and then on to Rankin Inlet, where I grew up? There's a lot of fucking shit that I don't know. I just want to connect the dots. I look at all my dad's brothers, how prevalent substance abuse is in the family. Did my uncles all go to residential school? No one wants to fucking talk about it. I don't want to raise any harsh feelings. I don't want anyone thinking, "Oh fuck, I don't want to be around Jordin. He's going to probably ask me those fucking questions again, so I'll just distance myself from him." A lot of our people hold grudges.

I know that my father was a star hockey player in the North in his teenage years, and that he went south to stay with family and play. He had an opportunity to try out for the New York Rangers, but at the last minute he didn't jump on the train to go to camp. He got cold feet. Why didn't he go? I don't know if he felt guilt or shame or regret about that.

Then there's my mom's story. I didn't know much about her life growing up, either. We never talked about it. I don't know almost anything about her family side. The only time we'd see her relatives was when we would go on holidays to Winnipeg. It was one day out of the year, hanging out with them.

My mother was an only child who grew up with an alcoholic father. She is of Ukrainian descent. But I don't know any details whatsoever. I'd ask her, "Mom, where did you grow up?" and she'd say Winnipeg or Dauphin, and that was the end of it. I remember meeting her grandmother—her "Baba." She had a couple of other aunts or uncles in Winnipeg who were in their seventies or eighties when I was a kid. I don't know their story. Her dad passed away before I was born.

My mother's mother, my Grandmother Doyle, was a chef and baker for a hotel in Churchill, then she moved to Baker Lake in Nunavut. I remember as a kid getting these goodie packages from Grandma Doyle—cookies and doughnuts, a whole box of fresh-baked goods. And that's pretty much it. Grandma passed away when I was ten or eleven years old.

(My mom's distant relatives all started coming out of the woodwork when I made the NHL. I had no time for them. I was too busy doing my own thing. A lot of them had moved to Ontario, so every time I was playing in Toronto, I'd get these random calls and my mom would be sending me emails saying, "You need to buy this many tickets." I'd put their names on the COD list, where they'd pay for their tickets at the gate. Then I'd look at my phone after the game and my mom would be ringing me: "What the hell, you didn't get them tickets?" Yeah, I fucking got them tickets, but they're paying for them. They wouldn't pay for them. So I was thinking, "Fuck you, I don't even know who the fuck you are." But I was getting heat from my mom because I was making all this money and she was complaining that I couldn't even buy ten fucking tickets. Well, ten fucking tickets—that's five thousand dollars.)

My mom and dad met in Churchill. My mom was a tourist who came up to see the whales and the polar bears. My dad and his brothers captured whales for zoos.

That's the minimal shit that I know about their life. I don't know how old they were when they met, or where else they might have travelled to. That has just been shut down.

So I had no idea whether my dad had been in a residential school or not. I always assumed that he was one of the lucky ones who hadn't been taken away. But reading that news story, I instantly, honestly felt pain. A sharp fucking jolt went through my body for my dad. And it connected everything. I wondered if this was part of why he is the way he is.

I've seen a few images, photos of the kids in front of the school. That was my dad, a little, lost kid looking off into space. Look at the sadness. When we're out on the land, does he ever reminisce? When he is sitting there in silence and looking off, is he thinking about what he's been through? Or has that just fucking been blanked out of his mind?

And then I look at my kids. I couldn't imagine the cops coming to us and saying, "Your kids got to go to this school, because it's better for them."

I didn't know it for sure, but I just felt like that had to be part of my dad's story.

And it instantly toned down my anger towards him, understanding a little bit about him. In my generation, it's a lot easier to get help, to see a therapist. For the older generation, that's a white man. They think, "They're going to try and tell me what I've got to be when I've already fucking been through that shit and lost everything—my culture, my tradition, my language. No fucking thanks."

A few days after getting home to Kelowna, I made one of my regular calls home. My mom answered the phone.

There were more stories about the residential schools in the news by then, and it was fresh in my mind. I watched a couple of documentaries to educate myself on what really went down and listened to some of the survivors who were fifty, sixty, seventy years old. That's my dad's era. When they talked about what happened to them, I was thinking, "Fuck, did that happened to my dad, too?"

"Hey, how are you doing?" I said to my mom. "Did you hear about the graves at the residential schools?"

"Yeah."

"Do you know if Dad went to one of those places?"

"Yeah, he went for one year in Chesterfield Inlet. Grade 10. But then he quit. And he's told me he don't remember nothing, and I didn't question it. He never talked about it again."

A whole wave of emotions ran right through me. I went silent thinking about my dad. What did he experience in that one year?

I wanted more from my mom. But she told me that Dad kept saying he didn't remember. At one point, they were offering compensation for residential school survivors and government people talked to my dad, she told me. (I had no idea that had happened.)

But he didn't get a payment because there wasn't enough detail.

That left so many questions I wanted to ask. Tell me about that whole year? Tell me how you got there and how you left? Did my dad purposely block what happened out of his mind?

But my mom cut the conversation off.

"Well, I got to go finish cutting the fish." She was at their cabin by the river, putting Arctic char out to dry.

I thought to myself, there's more to this, just by the way she ended that. My dad was there, so there was no way she wanted to talk about it in front of him.

Now I've got all of these fucking questions in my head. What's stopping me from asking them?

I realized I had to do it in person. I hadn't been in Nunavut in a year and a half because of the pandemic. You couldn't just go up there if you wanted to.

I had to find the courage within myself to move forward and have the guts to spit out those questions that could really define my father and define me as a human.

People always ask me, "How do you do it in sobriety? How do you stay sober?" When you really want something, you're going to find any way possible to do it. For me, at this point in my life, having that conversation with my dad is going to be even harder than getting sober. This is harder than leaving home at fourteen to play hockey. This is harder than being an enforcer in the NHL. To me, my dad is the most powerful and intimidating human being in the world, but yet the softest, most gentle giant.

I keep imagining what it is going to be like. I know there will be a lot of silence. "Dad, I love you . . . but I just, for my own mental health and my physical health, there's a lot weighing in my heart for you," I imagine myself saying. "Can you share some of your childhood experiences, chronologically, from the first time you remember? Can you help me process your life story? I've shared my life story with the world. And I feel that I have the right to know my own father's never-heard-before story, in order for me to be at peace with us, with our family. From my point of view, there's no judgment. I'm here. Your story's not going to change the way that I feel towards you. Good or bad, whatever happened, I'm just here to listen and to help us move forward as a family."

It will be just me and him. I feel there's parts of his life where he's very shameful, and that is fucking eating away at him, and he just buries it with booze. "Dad, it's okay," I want to say to him. "I fucked up many times because of my own decisions, and that had nothing to do with you guys. I'm a grown-ass man now and I have nothing to hide."

I don't think he'll say much at first. He'll talk about having a good life. And then he'll talk about the hockey. I feel like he's going to lean towards all the good things that happened to him.

But I've got to try and find out.

My dad is a very intelligent, kind, giving person. That soft side is what I see in him today, more than anything, because I'm not there physically to see those times when he turns into Mr. Hyde. That I want to forget about, but it's something I need to confront him with. I need to ask the question:

What the fuck happened to you?

3 We All Have Baggage

My last year in the Detroit Red Wings organization was very eventful, to say the least.

I got put on waivers right around Christmastime in 2013. We had the Winter Classic, against the Toronto Maple Leafs in the "Big House" in Ann Arbor, coming up that year, and I was very excited about what would have been my first outdoor NHL hockey game. Then, a couple of weeks before, the Wings' general manager, Kenny Holland, brought me into his office and told me they were going to put me on waivers.

It was the old story: "We're going to put you on waivers, but I guarantee that you'll get picked up." And you want to believe that. You think you're still going to play. It gives you a little burst of excitement, thinking that there's a very good chance of getting picked up by somebody else and getting a fresh start.

But that didn't happen. No other NHL team claimed me.

Everything kind of went downhill for me mentally after that. Having to go to the Wings' AHL team in Grand Rapids was a bit of a downer. After playing nine years in Nashville and hardly spending any time in the minors, it was a blow. And from then on, it was an uphill battle to get back into the NHL.

Kenny told me, "Just go down there. You'll be the first guy we're going to call up if we need another guy." Blah, blah, blah. Then, two days before the Winter Classic, they called up a couple other guys, but not me. I remember thinking, "What the fuck is going on here?" It pissed me off.

Jennifer and I stayed at our house in Detroit, and I drove back and forth to Grand Rapids. I'd wake up at 6 a.m. and hit the road for practice at nine o'clock, and then drive home afterwards. I watched the Red Wings play on TV while sitting on my living room couch. And I was thinking, "This ain't right."

It got to the point where I told Kenny to just fucking trade me. I knew I wasn't going to be the next guy in line to be called up. I knew I was still an NHL player. Trade me. Do something for me.

I played pissed off. Mentally, I wasn't in the right frame of mind. I remember them telling me I was going to play on the fourth line in Grand Rapids and they wanted me to take care of the other guys. Fuck you. Why am I going to do that when I know for a fact that none of these fucking guys are going to go to war with me? I knew I was riding solo.

I was getting pressure from Jen to walk into the office and raise hell—"Call your agent" and this and that. I brought all of that frustration into playing hockey. I was so pissed off that, during games, I would just fucking grab anybody I could and fight to blow off steam.

I remember one specific game when Jen came to watch. Right off the start, I got into a fight my first shift, and as soon as I got out of the box, I grabbed another guy and got into another fight.

Jen told me after the game that she walked out at that point.

"Why don't you just go back to Kelowna and plan our wedding?" I suggested. "I don't want to bring my frustrations home and you have to take the brunt of it and my shitty attitude."

She went back to B.C. and I moved to Grand Rapids, living in a hotel for three months, dealing with a lot of uncertainty.

I finished off the season not knowing what came next. I had been playing fourth-line minutes in the AHL. I knew I could still play, but my mind wasn't in the game. I not only played pissed off, I practised pissed off. As a veteran player, that's not the right attitude! But when you get fucked over, screwed over so many times, you've got to stick up for yourself.

Finally, I walked into Jeff Blashill's office—he was the coach in Grand Rapids then, and he's now coaching the Red Wings. "Look," I said, "at our first meeting you promised me that you were going to give me every opportunity. And here we are. I know I underachieved my expectations as a player. My chances of getting back in the NHL are pretty slim now, because of you guys wanting your younger guys to play more minutes."

Then I said, "Fuck you. Buy me out or fucking trade me this summer."

I still had a year left on my contract. But it got to the point where no one wanted to trade for me. The Wings finally bought me out right around the time of the draft.

Jen and I owned two properties then, one in Kelowna and one in Vancouver. We sat down and I said, "We've got a million-dollar mortgage on a house in Vancouver. I don't have a job. I don't know what's going to happen. We've got to sell." It was a sacrifice we had to make.

We got married that summer in Vancouver.

In rehab, they recommend that you not get into a serious relationship for at least a year into sobriety because there are a lot of triggers there. Prior to rehab, I thought I was always going to be a single, free-willed animal roaming around. But marriage was a turning point in my life in regards to growing up and being able to provide and be counted on as the man of the house.

When I first got out of rehab, I had a bunch of messages on my phone, and one of them was from Jen. I had met her way back in Brandon, when I was playing junior with the Wheat Kings. Before she got in contact, I can't even remember the last time I had talked to her. Probably a year or two prior, one of those times when the team was coming through town and I reached out and said, "Hey, are you around?"

I called her back and thanked her for her message. The Nashville Predators were coming to play the Canucks in Vancouver, and I happened to get cleared a few days before the

West Coast road trip so that I could practise with the team. We came out for four days and I invited Jen out for dinner. From that point on, we started to become closer.

She told me later that her initial thoughts were, "You're telling people you're a changed man, but this won't last." That was a hurdle. I had to prove myself to this person again. But it was a challenge I accepted.

We came back to play the Canucks in the second round of the playoffs that spring. Jen and I met up and went out for dinner a few times. After we lost to the Canucks, I was back to my place in Kelowna about a month later and I invited her to visit. She came out on the weekends and hung out.

When the next season was about to start and I was about to head back to Nashville, I actually asked her parents if they would approve of her moving down to the States with me.

That's when we kind of said, "Okay, are we a couple? Yeah? Let's do this."

We dived right in.

But we all have baggage. There are a lot of things Jen had to work on, because after getting sober, I saw life from a different perspective. She'd never seen me that way. There was a lot of adjusting.

Three or four months after moving to Nashville, Jen hit a wall. She was young, Nashville is a big entertainment town, and she was going out with the guys' girlfriends and wives to events and coming home fucking drunk, having a good time. She would tell me, "I don't have an alcohol problem, so I can have a few drinks." It stabbed me right through the heart. Why was the one person I was allowing into my life disrespecting me? Fuck that.

She actually went home to Vancouver for a few weeks and then called me and said, "I think I'm ready to come back."

Jen came back to Nashville and we worked through our shit. It's still a work-in-progress, and I thoroughly enjoy that, because I'm learning about myself through our therapy sessions.

A few months before the wedding, I had told my mom, "If you can't accept Jen being my wife, then there's going to be major changes. I'm not going to be around. If you disrespect my wife, I'm going to take my wife's side." I think that really shook her up because I was the only son they had left. Now I was moving on with my life

But my parents couldn't imagine letting go of their own kid. I think there was a big shift in their mindset towards me then. In my eyes, I had entered adulthood years before, but I think that was the point where they finally realized I was grown up.

There was a lot of excitement leading up to the wedding. It took some of my focus away from thinking about my hockey career. But I had to at least consider the possibility that I was never going to play again. Even throughout the wedding, I was still wondering what the fuck was going to happen now.

I got three of my buddies from back home to babysit my dad through the wedding, because they knew how to handle him. But I was worried about what he was going to do, who he was going to tell to fuck off after he started drinking. Plus, I had a lot of other people from Nunavut there, and that put a bit of a cloud over me because a lot of our people don't understand that drinking down south is different. Once they start, they don't take no for an answer.

Partying up north is totally different than partying down south. Up north, everybody knows everybody. Down south, people don't give a fuck who you are. You can't roll around thinking you're invincible like we do when we are in the North. When I came of age, I partied hard back home, but I knew everyone. We'd rough each other up, playing around amongst ourselves, but you knew your limits. Down south, you bump into someone at the bar and God only knows if they're going to be waiting for you outside at two in the morning with a fricking pistol or a knife.

I learned pretty quick to watch my surroundings and who I was around. But the people from up north are kind of like fish out of water when they come south, so it was a stressful couple of days leading up to the ceremony. I was tossing and turning in my bed thinking, Fuck, I hope nothing happens. This was the happiest day of my life. This was my wedding and the last thing I wanted was for this night to end with anyone out."

On the day of the wedding, all of Jen's family sat on one side and all of my family sat across the aisle— Quite a mix. There were also a bunch of past and current NHL players there from the BC area: Shea Weber, Ricky Vaitola, Luke and Brayden Schenn, Vern Fiddler, Kyle Turris, and more.

It was a great celebration. Everyone came together with happy tears. A lot of my cousins from the south took it upon themselves to look out for my friends and family from the

North, and I was very appreciative of that. I wanted to make sure everyone around me was taken care of and in good hands.

Usually when my family gets together, there's somewhat of a feud by the end of the night. But surprisingly enough, that didn't happen, either, and it was a lot of fun. It had been a long time since I saw both my parents smile like that. The joy. I felt like there was a lot of love in the air.

Then, after all the excitement was over, Jen and I, my mom and dad and my sister and her kids all drove back to Kelowna together from Vancouver. I rented a big van. And it was back to reality.

It was fucking nine o'clock at night and my dad had the gall to say to me, "Hey, can you stop at a liquor store?"

"Are you fucking serious?" I said.

It ticked me right off and kind of ruined the rest of the trip. This was supposed to be the happiest time you could have, and all he's fucking worried about is that he needs his next drink.

It was at that point that I threw in the towel for a while when it came to my parents. You guys are out of my life. There was minimal communication for months after that.

After the wedding, I was training hard and preparing myself for whatever happened. But I wasn't hearing anything.

It wasn't until the middle of August that I got a call from my agent saying that New Jersey was interested in giving me a PTO—a professional tryout. For a veteran player, that's the last resort. You get an invitation to training camp, but no guarantees unless you make the team.

A fucking PTO? You got to be kidding me. But it was my only offer on the table. I was lost mentally. Is this going to be it?

Lou Lamoriello, who ran the Devils organization, called me. "I have five guys coming in on PTOs, but I only have two spots," he told me.

Fuck. Talk about an uphill battle.

When I showed up in New Jersey for training camp, Lou called me into his office. "Toots," he said, "I've been watching you play for ten years now. I know what you bring to the table. So, prove to me that you want to be here. I know you're still an NHL player, but you've got to prove it."

I went in with the mindset of "Fuck everyone else; I'm coming here guns a-blazing." As far as my work ethic, what I bring into the dressing room, the positivity and all that—I was just going to be myself.

I didn't fight at all in camp. Lou said, "Do what you do—if you want to play your style, do it in exhibition games. You don't prove yourself against your own teammates. Why would you want to fight your teammates at training camp?" So I just showed up to work.

Jaromír Jágr was on that team that year. At that point, he had been playing in the league for twenty-some seasons. He came over to me and said, "Toots, I watch you every day. I want you to work me in the corners after practice. I know you work hard and I need that to stay in the league. I need someone to keep pushing me."

So, there's Jaromír Jágr, six foot four, 235 pounds, and there's me. Every day after practice, we'd do battle drills. Other guys would work on their shots, their tips, doing a little extra. Me and Jags would just work in the corners—dump the puck in, protect the puck, battle and work on conditioning. And I feel that those instances are where coaches sit back and watch and say, "You know, this kid really wants to be here, he wants to get better."

I didn't say a lot during camp. Prior to going to rehab, I used to do a lot of talking to my teammates. And in my drinking days, I made a lot of promises. But I knew that at that point in my career, my actions spoke louder than words. So I was a quieter guy in the dressing room. I worked hard on the ice, in the gym. Those are the traits that your teammates feed off of when they see somebody else putting in the extra time.

Two weeks into camp, Lou pulled me aside. "You earned it, buddy," he said. "You've got the contract." When I signed, I felt a lot of weight lifted off my shoulders.

The truth is that it was out of my control as to whether they thought I was the right fit for the team. And in fact, I'm not sure that Pete DeBoer, the coach of the Devils, ever did think I was the player he wanted. Right off the bat, he labelled me a fourth-liner. I was only going to play three to seven minutes a game. But I looked at it as an opportunity, and just buried my head and got to work.

Lou called me back into his office two or three times early that season. "Toots, just stick with it," he told me. "Things are going to get better. We need you on our team. Things will work out."

Two months went by and I was wondering what the fuck was going on. I was still in the lineup, but I was hardly playing.

And then, *boom*, over the Christmas holidays, Lou fired DeBoer and brought in Adam Oates and Scott Stevens to coach.

As soon as the coaching change happened, Lou called me into his office and said that this was what he'd been talking about. He was just waiting for the right opportunity to fire the coach and bring in Oatesy and Stevens as a buffer for the rest of the season.

Prior to them coming in, I had never met them. But when they arrived it was like a switch flipped on. It really loosened up the feel of the dressing room. They brought that sense of "Come to the rink with a smile on your face. We're not here to fucking bash you. We want you guys to all be successful." And everyone felt that. Everyone was treated equally. There was no fucking favouritism.

Both Oatesy and Stevens really believed in me and gave me an opportunity to expand my game. Oatesy especially knew the type of player that I was, knew that I could shoot the puck from any spot. Those are the kind of little things that he noticed because he wasn't far removed from playing.

Our first game after Christmas was on December 27 against the Rangers. We were in the dressing room at Madison Square Garden and Oatesy and Stevens walked in. There was no real pre-game meeting. They just said, "Here's the lines, boys. We're not going to get into any systems. We're going to roll all four lines. We don't give a shit who's up next for power play or penalty kill. We are just rolling with the punches."

We got killed, three-one.

The next morning at our video meeting, Lou walked in and started motherfucking everybody. Then he slapped in a twenty-minute highlight video of all of the eighties and nineties fights and brawls between the Rangers and Devils. We sat in there watching for forty minutes—he played the video twice. And then he let us have it.

"This is not Devils hockey. We don't get run over by anybody—especially the New York Rangers."

It got better . . .

I was put on the top line with Mike Cammalleri and Travis Zajac. I remember one game where we flew to Chicago to play the Blackhawks and I was on the ice for seventeen minutes. I was only conditioned to playing five minutes a game and I was thrown right into the fire.

During the second and third periods, Oatesy would come over to me and say, "Toots, just tell me when you want a break."

"No, I'm good. I'm good," I told him—because I didn't want to ruin that opportunity. I battled through.

After the game, on the bus from the United Center to the airport, I was so tired I passed out.

We were flying to Nashville to play the next night. I played another fourteen minutes and I passed out on the bus to the airport again. My body was exhausted.

But from that point on, things turned around. I knew deep down that if I just shut up and worked hard in practice, the opportunities would come. And that's what happened. I even got time on the power play.

Lou started hanging out behind the bench during games, too. I know this will surprise people, but Lou was a very cheerful coach. It was kind of like having a fan on the bench, which was pretty fucking cool to see. He gave off a lot of positivity, a lot of positive affirmation to the players that I would hear behind my back. It was a pleasant place to be and to play.

A couple of weeks into that season, I had pretty much set in stone that this was going to be my last year. The coaching staff at the beginning of the season didn't really believe in me. And now here I was, having a great time and playing an important role on the team. Sometimes you just have to be in the right place at the right time. But you still have to earn it.

I feel that in today's age, there are a lot of young players who don't want to work for what's given to them. And that extends back to being mentally aware of your work ethic, your attitude.

Everything is dependent on your performance on the ice, but that being said, what you do away from the rink also matters—the way you act around the arena, in the dressing rooms, all those little things. People don't realize how important it is as a teammate, even if you're a role player, to have a positive attitude.

If you look at star players, guys who are playing a lot of minutes, they've got a lot on their plate. You need that breath of fresh air in the dressing room. And that's where I find role players come in handy. When things weren't going their way, a lot of guys would look over at me and think, "Fuck yeah, I may think my life is shitty right now or I'm not doing my job, but look at Toots. He's coming to work every day with a smile on his face, putting his head down and just doing his job."

Lou Lamoriello gave me life and rejuvenated my love for the game. He's a straight-up person who cares about his players. And Lou was always honest with me. A lot of times, he'd come into the dressing room and ream me out in front of everybody. But afterwards, he would call me into his office and say, "You know, Toots, you're old school. You can take a little heat and not let it affect your mental state. I've got all these fucking young guys. If I give them shit, they'd be calling their agent or calling their parents. So I speak to veteran guys one way and the younger guys a different way. With you, I can make an example of you. Don't take it personally. It's just something that I think is good for our team."

After it happened, even the veteran guys would come up to me afterwards and say, "Fuck, that wasn't called for." They were trying to make me feel better.

"Guys," I told them. "It was called for."

4 I Couldn't Do That to Myself

It wasn't until after I signed with New Jersey that I really started to be okay with everything that had happened in my life and stopped blaming anyone else.

Back when I was in my cloud, just self-centred, it was all about me. I was sharing my wealth and buying the booze and getting everyone fucked up and creating wedges within families, all because of my antics.

Wives and girlfriends and kids were dreading the day that I came home to Rankin Inlet because they knew it was going to be a big piss-up.

After I got sober I had a lot of fear about going home. I had to face up to what I had done and do a lot of patching up of relationships, mending those gaps with my friends and their significant others. My best buddy, Troy, rode the bandwagon with me, and man, did I put his mom, his girlfriend at the time and their young daughter through a lot. I had to make things right with all of them.

I still had a lot of work to do on myself, too. Going through rehab and getting sober was only the beginning.

I didn't feel like I needed any outside resources to keep me sober, whether it was Alcoholics Anonymous meetings or anything else. I did go to AA in the beginning, for about a year after I got out of rehab, but for me it was too much of a Debbie Downer.

You're sitting in a room, listening to other people's stories. I could relate, but it was all negative energy that I felt. I still had my job, still had my family. I hit rock bottom in a different way than a lot of these people who had lost everything. And I felt like every time I left an AA meeting, it made me uncomfortable, because I had mixed feelings about my sobriety. Coming to those meetings actually made me want to fucking drink more. It made me feel like my life wasn't as fucked up as theirs.

I don't ever want to put myself in a higher category than anybody else, because we were all there for the same reason: alcoholism. We all have different stories that we can relate in different ways, but I was forced to go to AA. It was part of my program. I did what I had to do.

But to be honest, I couldn't even tell you the twelve steps. I couldn't relate and I couldn't connect.

I also worked with a therapist in Nashville during my first year after rehab. They had me writing down my life experiences, but I sugar-coated everything. I just wanted to keep the therapist at bay, to be in control. And I felt like I needed that control to keep functioning. I thought I had done all of the work I needed to do when I was in rehab.

I was wrong about that.

That transition from using to sober, and from single to married, wasn't easy.

A few times, I caught myself and had to realize, "Oh, shit, I'm married." Your male instincts when you're young and in the professional sports world are that you want to push your limits a little bit to see if you've still got it in you to pick up girls. It's just what you're used to. Then, all of a sudden, big change. Those were two significant changes in my life: sobriety and marriage. Two huge accomplishments that it takes years to become comfortable with—especially in a world of instant gratification. Swipe the phone and everything is at your fingertips. But there was a point where I realized, "Fuck, I married my dream lady. I don't want to fuck that up."

As a player, suddenly I was dealing with no social interaction on the road. And social interaction was everything to me, because it kept my mind off of everything else that was going on. The biggest thing that helped me go to sleep at night was knowing that there was someone lying next to me and I was safe—a female figure was next to me, comforting me. Then it was okay to close my eyes.

I had that with my brother growing up. We slept side by side until he left home.

That's one of the reasons I got addicted to the sleeping pill Ambien. I would ask the other guys, "What are the boys doing for dinner?" Lucky fuckers, they were out having a bottle of wine while I was stuck sitting in my hotel room, ordering room service. Then, right after room service, I'd pop a couple of Ambos trying to battle it, to feel that drunken stage that I used to be in, where you're all wonky.

And then I'd pop another one to really put me out.

I started doing that right after I got out of rehab. I went to our team doctor and said, "Lookit, I'm having a lot of trouble sleeping at night," and he handed over the pills.

That became my new routine—painkillers and Ambien. The painkillers weren't the strong shit, like opioids. It was Advil or hydrocodone. The stronger shit made me feel all fucked up, and I didn't like that. But I thought Ambien was the greatest thing for me. In that first year of my sobriety, that's what put me to sleep every night.

And then slowly, over time, I started taking four Ambien instead of one or two. I was falling asleep at ten o'clock, waking up at midnight to go piss, and then fucking popping another one or two. I'd get up in the morning and feel like shit, like I was hungover.

I definitely wasn't the only one doing it. I remember watching my teammates land in a city on a road trip and they'd be popping Ambien on the bus coming in from the airport. I remember thinking, "Are you guys fucking serious?"

That's when I realized Ambien was getting to be a problem in the whole league—it was kind of the Ambien era in the

NHL. And guys were mixing booze with it. That's a fucking deadly combination, and it was common back then. It actually scared me to look at my teammates, stumbling before we even got off the fucking bus to our hotel.

There was a lot of bullshitting going on amongst the players, convincing the doctors that they were having sleeping problems so they'd have the pills in their back pocket for a rainy day. Guys were sharing pills—that shit was happening all the time. I never had trouble getting them because if I was out, I knew ten of my teammates had them.

For a while I was rooming with Wade Belak on the road. We weren't in the lineup much and we were just getting bag-skated every day in practice.

Belak was a huge mentor of mine because of the way he carried himself. But he liked his Ambien, too. And we'd crush six, seven of them, pour them in our drink, throw money on the nightstand, and whoever stayed up the latest got the money.

After one of those episodes, I woke up in the morning and saw that our room had been torn upside down. I had no memory of what we had done the night before. I thought, "What the fuck? This is not right." I was abusing it. And I quit cold turkey right then and there.

I remember telling Beaker the next night, "Sorry, Bud, but I'm out as far as these games and stuff." There were a lot of moody nights for me because of that transition. I felt terrible. I remember thinking, "Fuck, Jen doesn't deserve this."

Not having the Ambien to put me out brought back a lot of emotions at night. My head was fucking racing, but I figured I had already gotten over the biggest hurdle of my life when I quit drinking. I knew that I had an addictive personality and this was something that I had to control right away.

Eventually I became comfortable without any substances in my body, but I don't judge what other guys did. You do your own thing. We're all fucking adults here.

As the years passed, cannabis edibles started to become popular in the league and mostly took the place of sleeping pills—especially after they were legalized. I feel like that's what most guys are on now. A few years ago, before everything was legal, it was a hidden thing. You'd go on a road trip down to Colorado, one of the first places where weed was legalized, and guys would head straight to the dispensary and load up with edibles for the rest of the season. Even with it being legalized, I feel like it's still kind of a hidden code among players.

In my eyes, when I was growing up, weed was always way worse than alcohol. Did I try it? Of course I did, but I wanted to be in control of my body at all times. I didn't like that out-of-body feeling. I never smoked weed or did cocaine when I was partying. Booze was my drug. And the first time I tried an edible, I thought, "I need this out of my body right now. Who the fuck likes this feeling?"

Around the time edibles started becoming common around the league, it was also a transition point where guys stopped going out together while on the road. Everyone was doing their own thing. Fewer and fewer and fewer guys were even going out for dinner together. They would rather just be in their own space, order room service, stay home in their hotel, eat a couple edibles and crash out.

That wasn't only about the cannabis—it was part of a shift in the whole hockey culture. Things really changed after the 2012–13 lockout, when we lost a big part of the season.

During the first years of my career, it was part of the hockey culture to socialize with your teammates. On almost every fucking road trip, as soon as we got to the hotel, everyone chucked their bags, threw on a pair of jeans and off we went to happy hour. There was always a place to go. That's how we bonded. We all went out.

Happy hour led to a few afternoon drinks to dinner to a couple of bottles of wine. Then, after dinner, you were going to the club to scope it out. We'd get back to the hotel for the ten or eleven o'clock curfew.

There were no secrets back then. Everyone would show up the next morning at the rink and no one would talk about what happened the night before. Guys were a lot closer off the ice.

Towards the end of my drinking days, when it was getting really bad, I learned how to not drag any of my teammates down to my level. I always knew that I could battle through the mental grind of a practice when I was hungover. But a lot of guys I hung out with couldn't do that without being exposed. Guys would have shitty practices and the coach would say, "What the fuck is up with you? Where were you last night?" So now they were in shit because I made them hang out with me the night before while I was in the clear, not getting noticed, having a shitty practice. Eventually I decided I didn't want to get any of my teammates into trouble, so I would go by myself and call friends of mine away from the game who were in the music industry or the bar scene.

I would go to places where only locals would hang out. I started venturing off to places where you would never, ever think you would go. I remember many times being in this little dive bar by my house. No one in their right mind would go to these places other than locals who had been alcoholics for forty years. I'd walk in and no one knew what I did. They just knew I would buy beers for everyone.

The game started to shift after the lockout. Social media was on the go and it almost turned a lot of guys into hermits. But the main thing was that the young generation of players have no fucking clue about enjoying your time in The Show—you can have fun and still work when it's time to go to work.

Guys started fucking throwing each other under the bus. If someone was out and had a shitty practice the next day, they'd tell the coach, "I wasn't the only one out. So-and-so was out." When I was starting out, you never did that. You took the fucking blow yourself. If something happened, if there was a kerfuffle at the bar and only one name was mentioned, that guy took the heat for everyone else. Now, if a player gets in trouble, he rats out his teammates to prove he wasn't the only one involved. And that's where the divide started moving on the ice. How do you go fight for your teammate when he just fucking threw you under the bus in front of your coaches?

———

I was in Kelowna when I heard that Wade Belak died. He hung himself in a hotel room in Toronto while he was shooting the TV show *Battle of the Blades*. No one will ever know for sure whether it was suicide or some kind of misadventure. When it happened, a lot of people automatically connected it to the death of a couple of other NHL enforcers, Derek Boogaard and Rick Rypien.

My first thought was, "How could this be?" I was his room-mate and I didn't fucking suspect a thing. I thought I fucking knew the guy. We had a lot of personal conversations, me and Beaker. I thought I was pretty close to him. And then, fucking *boom*. What the fuck just happened?

I felt like I was reliving the experience I had when my brother passed away. All those same emotions. What could I have done? Was I a good teammate? A lot of questions. But like I tell a lot of people, when it comes to suicide, sometimes you may never know.

Beaker was the light of the room. The guy was full of piss and vinegar. He always had that big smile on his face. He was the one who brought everyone on the team together. And he was a guy who had been through the meat grinder. I feel like a lot of players who've never been in an enforcer's shoes will never understand the pain, the agony, the self-destruction internally, while still wanting to be around the game, even if you're a fourth-line player. You do whatever it takes to stay there.

Wade was the definition of a great teammate all around. He was a family guy, he had a wife and kids. I loved the way he carried himself.

But with mental health, you never know. If you don't know how to speak up, shit can happen. It took me a lot of years to be able to talk. I couldn't imagine what it's like for people without resources or outlets. And you might think, "It's never going to happen to me, even in those darkest days," but I know there was at least one time when I thought about following the same path.

Right after I got out of rehab, I was with the Preds in San Jose for a game against the Sharks. We were staying at the Hotel Valencia. It was kind of funny, because that hotel was one of the last places that I partied, slamming open the mini-bar fridge and downing whatever was in there.

It was ten o'clock at night, I was angry and frustrated, and I was looking out the window and asking myself, "Why am I even doing this? You guys testing me every fucking day, not letting me on the ice. Why aren't you on my side? Where's that nurturing part that I need right now?"

Suicide was definitely in my mind because I wanted to be with my brother in that moment.

Like other times when that thought came to me, it gave me a stabbing pain in my stomach. When I felt that pain, I realized that I couldn't do that to myself. There was a lot of talk in my own head, but I just couldn't comprehend following through.

Thank God for my sobriety. If I had been fucking drunk and incoherent, I probably would have done it.

5 I Had to Tell the Truth

The biggest part of coming to terms with my life was writing my book, *All the Way*, in 2014. It took me a while to get comfortable with the whole idea, and then it just clicked for me and I thought, "Fuck it, it's time to get that shit off my shoulders."

When the book was all said and done, it was almost like a sigh of relief. I give a lot of credit to Stephen Brunt for getting me to open up. I remember him asking the same questions over and over and over and saying, "Is that the truth? Is that the whole story?" The more you think about them, things start to come in your head. When we were writing the book, I had a lot of question marks in me and I was fearful. That little kid in me would come out and think, "Well, I shouldn't say this because I'm going to get in shit." But as time went on, I became more comfortable in my skin and allowed myself to really be vulnerable. It really helped me open up and see what else was out there in the world. Finally I got to the point where I was ready to tell the whole truth.

It was a turning point in my life—not only for me, but for my family. It was a chance to really understand what we've all been through. I don't resent anybody for my life experiences. I'm grateful for everything I've endured. By allowing me to dive into a lot of deep-rooted issues, the book has only been beneficial.

But I was also scared shitless when the book came out. I remember reading the manuscript and thinking, "Holy shit, this is everything that I said! Now I've got to go back and confirm a lot of the stories with people that I grew up with." I remember reaching out to a number of them and them asking, "Why are you asking me these questions?" It was a very foreign experience for a lot of people that I grew up surrounded by. "Hey, remember this? Did this happen?" Those were stories that you put in the back of your head and tried to forget about. It was difficult for all of us to talk openly about what had happened in our lives.

Was I worried about how people would react to the book when it came out? Oh fuck, yeah. That was my biggest concern—especially my family and especially my mom. I knew I was going to get a fucking earful when she was done reading it.

My sister, Corinne, has always been kind of a mother figure for me. She was scared for me when the book was coming out and scared about the possibility of shit hitting the fan. When she read the book, her first reaction was to ask me, "Are you sure you want to say all of that stuff? I'm scared something might happen."

Of course she was thinking about suicide.

That has been the mentality for our people for a lot of years—don't overreact because if you scold your kids too much, they're going to do themselves in. What my sister thought was that maybe the book would push Mom or Dad over the edge and they might kill themselves. Are they going to do themselves in because of it being so shameful? I knew that there was no way that they would understand I wasn't just trying to expose them—and I did expose them a little bit. But I hoped it would turn into a positive conversation for us. Although they didn't want to believe it, they knew deep down inside that whatever stories I shared were true.

I was brutally honest with Corinne. I told her that in order for me to keep going and for us to come together at the end of all this, I had to tell the truth. In the end it would only make us stronger. And I said to my mom, "I love you guys no matter what. This book is a way for us to heal as a family."

When my mom called me about it, it caught me off guard.

"I read the book," she said. My heart just stopped. I figured I was going to get beat down. But it was actually a very positive conversation. We went through the book and she asked me some questions. And then she said, "I hope that you still love us after everything that you said. You know some of the stuff that you said didn't happen."

I just let her talk; I wasn't going to fucking argue. "Hopefully this will help a lot of people," she said. But she was referring to other people, not us.

Mom told me that Dad hadn't read it yet, but he was going to.

I waited a few weeks and didn't hear from them. Finally I had to call Mom and ask her.

"Yeah, I think he opened up a couple pages," she said. "And then he put it down."

Outside of my family and my friends, I was worried about how the community in Rankin would react to the book. We were always viewed as one of the successful families in town. People looked up to us. They would think, "They're so lucky—they've got everything." Now my book was coming out and it felt like everyone in town was thinking, "Holy shit, I didn't know that about them. It was all a secret." Pull the blinds and shut the doors.

How was everybody going to view my parents after this? I assume that, for the first two or three years after it came out, my parents kind of hid behind closed doors a lot because they didn't want to face the fact that pretty much everybody in our community had read the book. They didn't want to deal with the reality of people judging them.

Now that a few more years have gone by, you know what? Families that are close to us who have read the book turn out to have dealt with the same shit that we did. It's not news. Even my parents' friends, after reading the book, have said they have looked back on their own lives and their own home environments in a different way. People actually started to look at themselves in the mirror.

But the reaction wasn't all positive. There were some people— mostly more distant family members—who said, "How dare you expose your family like this?" I didn't give a shit what they thought. I decided to do this to help myself heal and to help our family heal, not to expose anyone or express resentment about my parents in any way. I did it to come to a realization as a family of the mistakes we had made and move forward. And if you don't like it, then fuck you, guys. Who gives a fuck what other people think?

I held my head up high and I was proud of what I did. I came to the realization that I can't make everyone happy. There are going to be fucking naysayers whether you like it or not. You have to manage those comments and the judgment directed towards you. But you can't control what other people say or do towards you. All you can control are your own actions, and I was at a point in my life where I had to come clean with everything to move forward.

My first trip back to Rankin after the book was published was weird. It had been out for a year by then. I remember landing in town and paying close attention to a lot of people's reactions when they saw me. Some of my buddies didn't know how to bring up the book because they didn't want to bring up their pasts. But every time I was around them, I would talk about my book. And slowly it became normal for people to say, "Yeah, me too. I can totally relate." My best friends in Rankin Inlet— Troy, Pujjuut, Warren, Wayne—all reacted the same way. They said, "Holy shit, I felt like I was reading my own childhood stories." Looking back on our lives, it really confirmed for me why a lot of us were constantly around each other at all hours of the day and night. It was because we didn't want to be home—but no one shared what was going on behind closed doors. I think the book definitely helped my close buddies understand that it wasn't our fault. It wasn't so much that there was no one to blame for our parents' actions, but understanding where their actions came from in adulthood, why they were the way that they were. The past trauma. As a kid, you don't fucking know that shit.

Outside of my family and the people in my hometown, I think what most surprised me was the reaction to the book in the hockey world. After it came out, all kinds of people approached me and thanked me for sharing my story—referees, linesmen, game-day staff in almost every building I went into, the coaching and training staffs from other teams—they all said they could identify with what I had written.

The coolest thing was players on opposing teams who would talk to me right in the middle of a game during a TV time out or before a faceoff, saying, "Hey, thank you, Toots, for sharing your story. I can relate." Obviously, the book hit home for a lot of people.

When I was playing in New Jersey, Montreal came to town for a game. We were practising on a Thursday afternoon and the Canadiens were scheduled to come on right after us. I saw Carey Price and gave him a copy of the book. Carey and I have known each other for a long time.

That night—actually, at four o'clock on Friday morning—Carey texted me. "Hey Toots I just finished reading your book. I couldn't put it down." He stayed up all night before a game and read my book, and he had to play the next night.

He still played—and of course he absolutely killed us on two hours of sleep.

I heard from a lot of Indigenous players—Jordan Nolan, Arron Asham, Gino Odjick, Stan Jonathan, Ethan Bear, Brady Keeper—who reached out by text or through social media. The book seemed to really open up the doors for a lot of Indigenous athletes to share their own stories, and for non-Indigenous people to realize that a lot of us have come from not-so-good places and yet found a way to survive and succeed.

I heard from some of my past coaches and general managers, including Barry Trotz and David Poile from my days in Nashville. I've stayed very close with them. I remember the first time I saw Trotsy after the book came out, and he gave me a wink and a big hug. "I'm proud of what you did in your book," he told me. "You needed to do that to move forward in your life." Being around Trotsy and Poile has always been a real comfort for me. I can't believe they're still around after all that I put them through. When you go through what I did, you find out who your true friends are pretty damned quick.

And then there were all of the people who aren't in hockey and who I don't know personally, who contacted me through social media. There were tons of them who reached out to say they'd read the book four or five times and kept finding different parts that they could relate to.

A lot of Indigenous readers would leave comments thanking me for writing the book and for the courage I showed by being open and honest. "Thank you for leading the way. Thank you for opening those doors for me."

When you share life experiences from the dark side of our upbringing, it brings out the realization that no one else is going to fix the situation unless you take control of it. Playing the victim is over; it's time to make a stand. I feel like my book has played a role in helping people do that.

Every time I have a speaking engagement, people bring their books with them for me to sign. I wish I had ten or fifteen minutes for every person who comes up to me and says they can relate to this or that part of the book. I wish I had more time for them to share, to really help them heal.

It's tough to talk to someone who has never experienced growing up in a dysfunctional home or with alcoholic parents or around substance abuse. A lot of the people who read my book are in adulthood and have never talked openly about their experiences. They don't know how to talk about the emotional and physical abuse they have been through. They are very nervous about revealing themselves in front of everyone. But that's the first step. I give a lot of credit to the people who have had the courage to share their stories with me. That cracks the door open a little bit to maybe make them feel confident enough to delve into their childhood traumas and experiences.

To get past it, you've got to be able to expose it, take it on with full force and communicate about it. Verbalize your experience with someone you can trust. That's the biggest thing—finding that one person who you can share your story with, someone to just sit there and listen. Especially for a lot of us men—we don't need answers or solutions right in that moment, we just need to be heard. We need to get to that point of verbalizing what we're feeling, and we don't know how to do that.

I received hundreds and hundreds of messages on social media. Many of them came from Indigenous people all across Canada. Some of them just posted a picture of the book. They didn't need words to express what they were feeling.

There was one I received that wasn't from an Indigenous person, but it meant a lot to me because I thought of the teachers who were so important in my life.

Hi Jordin. My name is Gillian and I am a first-year teacher. I am from Toronto but chose to teach in Cambridge Bay, Nunavut, for my first year. I am currently teaching a Grade 2 class. Just before the holiday break I found your book in the shelves of my colleague's classroom. Over the break I read the book and I just wanted to say thank you. My first five months teaching in the North has taught me so much and more than anything, I've been learning from my students about their lives and what it's like growing up here. I want to thank you because your book gave me more insight to what these kids' lives are like—the good and the bad. It was encouraging and inspiring. I'm sure you have been a positive role model for a lot of Inuk kids. Thank you for being someone they can relate to and showing them that dreams are possible.

6 Only You Can Do It

At our year-end meeting after my first season in New Jersey, Lou told me, "Good for you. You did everything that we wanted you to do. You deserve to be in the NHL. I want to sign you for next year, but we're not going to publicize your signing for a couple more weeks, because there's kind of a lot of stuff going on."

A couple of weeks later, he did sign me. And two days after that, Lou resigned as GM and president of the New Jersey Devils and went to the Toronto Maple Leafs.

He called me a couple of weeks later. "Toots, I wanted to make sure that you were signed," he said. "I didn't want to leave you hanging in the weeds all summer, not knowing if you were going to get another contract, if the new general manager was going to sign you or if you were going to be signed by somebody else. I personally wanted to sign you before I left."

I thought that was really nice of him, and a very kind gesture. He's a guy I respect a lot. He's had to deal with a lot of players in similar situations to mine, that have gone through the program, that have dealt with substance abuse. So he cared about me.

Away from the ice, Jen and I promised each other that we were going to start to really enjoy our life and not let the game consume us. We lived in Hoboken, New Jersey, right across the river from Manhattan, and got to experience New York City quite a bit. After practice we'd go right into the city and explore and forget about the whole hockey life for a few hours. I think that really helped me focus on loving the game again. When I left the rink, I left everything that was going on there and didn't bring it home.

The first years of marriage are all puppy love. You're still excited and talking about babies and stuff. Well, that conversation was quite interesting, because I didn't think I was quite ready to be a dad and take on that responsibility. I still needed to fix myself. I still needed to work on things.

I feel like I went into marriage blind, because I didn't have a role model to look up to—especially a male figure. I watched my teammates who were married and had kids. I saw how they carried themselves professionally. When we had team events, I observed how they were with their wives. There was a lot of affection going on. I had never seen that growing up—holding hands, kissing, pecks here and there in public. That was very foreign to me. And Jen's the total opposite. She needs touch, and I just never experienced that from watching my dad. I had to get over that hurdle and be comfortable being close to my wife and not feeling like it was weird.

There were also moments where I would hear myself raise my voice and realize, "I've got to fucking take a few steps back or I've got to leave the room." There were a lot of times when I would stop myself and apologize to my wife because I would catch myself and realize, "Fuck, that's my dad speaking to my mom."

You are what you are surrounded with. As a child growing up, when you're in an environment where there's a lot of chaos, a lot of dysfunction, your mind and body tend to be programmed around that. You learn inadvertently after witnessing it so many times over and over again for years.

In my relationships I tend to revert to what I know and what I saw. I saw my dad many times raise his voice and become frustrated with my mom or with people around him when he was under the influence. There was a lot of yelling.

When my emotions start to ramp up, I tend to try and escape that situation, whether it's by leaving the room or going outside. A lot of times I feel guilt inside because those are the situations where I have to stand up and be a better man than what I know and what I revert to. I feel like I'm abandoning my wife when she needs my support the most. To this day I tend to revert to leaving the room and taking a couple of deep breaths to calm myself down. There are many times when I've gotten frustrated with my kids or Jen and just left the situation because I knew that the Barney in me was going to come out and I didn't want them to see that.

It's frustrating. I'm still learning how to articulate my thoughts and put them into words in that moment. I tend to put things in the back of my head and forget about them. Then the blow-up would happen while I played hockey. I used hockey to release a lot of my frustration. I fought a lot. I was aggressive on the ice. I didn't want to hurt my family at home, so I let it out at the rink, taking liberties and taking penalties, and I hurt my teammates that way because of my off-ice antics.

I was a loose cannon at the rink. That's what the fans wanted to see, and that's all I cared about. I didn't understand why I was limited in ice time—it was because I was a threat to my own teammates. We would be in a tight game with ten minutes left and I'd be on the bench because they didn't know if I was going to take a stupid penalty. In sobriety, when I had a lot more clarity, I learned to pick and choose my spots and not hurt my team.

Off the ice, I was silent a lot. I feel bad that I put Jen in a situation where there was no communication between us. She was constantly walking on eggshells and didn't want to piss me off.

As much as I became aware of the destructive tendencies that I had learned from my dad, there were also some positive things I could take from him. He always provided for our family. There was always food on the table. On the land, he taught us a lot. I felt like I could use some of that in my marriage, and hopefully someday show my kids.

There was a lot for me to absorb about marriage, while still trying to be my own person. I had to realize that it wasn't all about me anymore. I had to make sure our household was a safe place. That took some time, because Jen knew the Jordin Tootoo prior to sobering up, and it was almost like she was waiting for a ticking time bomb to go off, waiting for me to pick up and start drinking again.

And there were a few moments where I felt that life would be easier if I was back drinking. I threatened to do it multiple times because I didn't know how to communicate with Jen. After all the therapy sessions, you think you've done enough that you've got to the bottom of everything. But as you peel all those layers back, rewiring your brain, learning how to articulate your thoughts and put them into words, it's tough. A lot of times, I would just throw my hands up. My whole life, I've been controlled by someone, ever since I was a little kid. And now it felt like my wife was trying to control me.

"Fuck it. I'm going to go and start drinking again." I said that and I threatened it, but deep down inside, I knew I wasn't going to actually physically pick up a drink. But if I scared Jen, she would back off.

I remember the night I came closest to falling off the wagon. It was during the off-season and we were at our old house in Kelowna. I was doing dishes in the kitchen, it was about six o'clock on a weekend night, and something Jen said just set me off. I don't remember exactly what it was, but I threw my hands up in the air and told her, "Fuck this. I can't handle this anymore. I'm out of here. I'm going to fucking drink my face off."

I purposely left my phone on the island in the kitchen as I stormed out of the house. Jen asked me where I was going, but I didn't answer her.

I went and grabbed a bite to eat down the road at a restaurant. I was sitting there at the bar, looking at all the fucking bottles and seeing Grey Goose, which was my drink. I stared that bottle down for probably fifteen minutes.

Then something clicked inside of me. I knew I was done. If I was to ever pick up and start drinking again, my marriage would have been over, my career would have been finished, everything that I had worked for up to that point would have been all thrown away.

When I got back to the house and I saw Jen curled up in a ball, I thought, "What the fuck am I doing? She doesn't deserve this." I made a promise to myself that night that I would never threaten her again with picking up a drink.

Looking back, I understand what Jen's intentions were. She was trying to better me as a human and push me. But I felt pressure from her, and I had so much pressure from my family and from the hockey world that it felt like everyone was ganging up on me.

It wasn't until years into therapy that everything started to click and her understanding of me grew. We had two totally different lives. She couldn't relate to what I was trying to explain to her. A lot of times she would say, "Get over it"—shit like that. And it's way more complicated than that.

We all have needs, and we've got to be able to meet in the middle and create an environment where we're able to sit down in front of each other and talk about everything. I feel now like we're starting to get to that point. I never had a voice when I'd communicate with Jen. Sometimes we just want to be heard. That's why I feel a lot of Indigenous people are afraid to open up a can of worms to somebody—because they're going to be told what they've got to do to fix themselves. Can you just fucking hear me out?

I never really dived into my childhood experiences with Jen for the first five years of sobriety because I thought I had already worked through that shit. And then, over time, slowly, there were moments when I would go silent because Jen raised her voice and that scared little boy inside of me would put up walls and remove myself from the situation. I would walk away or tell her to get out of my face and give me some space. I just didn't know how to communicate what I was actually feeling.

I feel like now those breakthroughs are starting to happen, where I can honestly say, "Hey, can we have a little space here?" Whereas before, it'd be like, "Get the fuck out of my face, I don't want to hear." And I'd leave, and that would leave Jen lost.

Ten years into sobriety and seven years into marriage, it's still a work-in-progress. A lot of people, when they find out we're in couples therapy, their instinct is to ask, "Are you guys okay? Is your marriage okay?" It's great, but the therapy is helping us totally understand each other, with a mediator who doesn't take any sides and listens to both of us talk. A lot of times at home, I felt like I didn't have the room to talk because I felt like Jen was only hearing the first fucking five words that came out of my mouth and then she was already thinking to reply and then cutting me off. That's when I'd just throw my hands up in the air and think, "I can't even explain or tell you my story." But I feel like now, our communication lines are so much better.

A lot of ex-teammates and former NHL players come to visit me in Kelowna during the summertime. We'll be out on a boat on Friday afternoon, and they're drinking, and I'll tell them I have to leave to go to therapy. "What? Come on? What the fuck do you need therapy for?" I tell them I will be in therapy for the rest of my life and I have no problem with that.

Some of them, who know my story, also come to me, looking for advice.

I remember one current player who went out on the town in Kelowna with me, and he wound up half-cut. "Fuck, Toots," he said, "how do you do this? I need to get on the wagon."

I'm not the kind of guy who will force the situation, but if someone is willing to talk, I will share with him what I've experienced. People are scared of the unknown. By sharing my history and my past, it really helped that player get over the hump and say, "Fuck everyone else. I've got to do this for me and my family." He had to figure that out for himself.

We had a conversation a couple of days before he went into rehab, and I think that helped him stop worrying about what everyone else was going to think. I told him I'd much rather sacrifice thirty days getting help so I can be with my kids at six in the morning for the rest of my life. That's exactly what I told him. On Sunday morning, when your daughters are nagging at you to come and play, you're never going to do that when you're fucking hungover. Look at it from that perspective of being able to be with your kids and putting in the time that you missed during the season, not being able to be there. I think it really sunk into his head. The guilt of knowing that he was that person at six in the morning who said, "Go wake up your mom. I'm too tired." I've been there—not with my kids, because I stopped drinking before they were born, but with family that came to town. I'd sleep until one or two in the afternoon.

And he's not the only player who approached me. I don't want to say a lot of it was influenced by me, but I know for a fact that a lot of guys have looked at life from a different perspective after that conversation.

I'm straight up with the guys: It's fucking willpower. If you want to do something, only you can do it. No one can do it for you. It's hard when you're in the public eye and people are pulling you in different directions. I've seen it first-hand.

7 We Were Venturing into Unknown Territory

After I re-signed with the Devils, I knew we were good for another year. So that's when we decided to start trying to have a baby. We got pregnant in August of that summer.

It didn't really hit me until about the five-, six-month mark, where you could start to see Jen's belly pop out. It was a very exciting time knowing that I was actually going to be a father. During my single years, I was always afraid to knock somebody up. That was a fear of mine. Knowing I was going to be a dad was a shift in my life in terms of maturity. I changed my life so that I could create a healthy environment for my family.

When our daughter Siena was born, I was instantly in protective mode. I was right beside Jen for the birth, and when the nurses took Siena away to weigh her, my first instinct was for my guard to go up and to think, "Hey, what are you doing with her?"

I'm a pretty heavy sleeper, but in the first few months of her life, any little movement, like if she was rummaging around in the crib next to our bed, and I was up right away, making sure that everything was okay.

Both Jen and I were venturing into unknown territory. A lot of outside sources tell you a lot of different things about being a parent. I remember sitting there with Jen as all our friends and family gave us tips. Sometimes we got consumed by all the information. I remember saying we should hear everyone out, but in the end we should just do our own thing.

It took time for us to accept and believe that we could do it on our own. There were moments where we were just so exhausted, I wondered if we could ever handle another kid.

In my sobriety, being physically and emotionally there for my wife was a huge transition for me. I had to nurture my wife *and* our little one. I never got that as a kid myself, so I didn't know if I was doing the right thing. But I just tried to be present.

And at that point in my hockey career, I'd been playing for eleven, twelve years in the league, but for the first time, my mindset shifted to family first. And I was looking forward to the next chapter in my life.

A lot of my teammates had kids while they were still playing and their kids got to watch their dad play in the NHL. I kind of missed out on that, but I would take being present as a father every day over being on the road and gone and missing out on their childhood.

Being around Jen's family really opened up my eyes in regards to love and affection. I feel like I overcompensated with my kids in giving that, at the expense of giving it to my wife. We've had conversations where Jen said, "I feel like I'm kind of left out. It'd be nice to get some of that love and affection that you give the kids." That was an aha moment for me. I realized I was walking in my dad's shoes. I had never seen my dad kiss my mom or hug my mom. I told myself that as the kids got older, I wanted to show them what kind of man they should expect when they go find one for themselves, after watching me and how I am with Jen: a caring, loving husband.

I know too many people who had their parents split up when they were younger and it fucked them up. You look at the people who have addiction issues, and 85 to 90 per cent of them didn't have a male figure to look up to. One of my biggest goals in life is to be present with my kids and be open and show them what kind of man they deserve by watching their dad and mom.

When I was playing in Nashville, I remember that we had a fathers' road trip. Every one of us had to stand up in front of the whole team and introduce our dad.

One of my teammates would always talk about how his dad thought he was always right and better and the best—one of those cocky fucking guys. That day, the player got up and introduced his dad, and his last line was: "You always told me when you have kids, you raise them to be a better version of yourself. Dad, I can honestly say, I'm fucking better than you." I guess what he meant was that he had made it to the NHL and his dad had never made it.

The whole room went fucking dead silent. Imagine being told by your dad for your whole life that you're not fucking good enough, and then standing up and making that statement in front of an audience.

Would I ever tell my parents that I was a better version of them? No. Because that's disrespectful. That bond is important.

But everyone has a breaking-point.

I think when I heard that, it drove me to be a better husband and a better father for my kids than my dad was. But I still take a lot of his qualities and use them to improve myself, rather than focus on the negative shit.

A lot of people just dwell on the negative all the time and think, "Well, fuck, my parents passed that down to me." Yeah, but you've also got to give your parents credit for doing the best they could with what they knew. I don't resent my parents for anything. I'm actually grateful for everything that I've experienced.

The moment my wife gave birth to our daughters, I realized that nothing else in this world matters more than protecting those two precious little girls. All of my selfishness disappeared. I was going to do everything in my power to make sure they are safe, they are loved, they feel wanted and they are going to be whoever they want to be. I'm going to support them on any journey that life takes them.

I know that everything I do is for them. It kind of turned that page. There was a time when everything I did was for me. Now everything I do is for my wife and my family. In the years past, I looked after my immediate family and did whatever it took. But now, having my own family, I came to the realization that I've got to make sure that they're looked after first before I can look after anybody else.

It's been an amazing journey, being able to watch our daughters grow up into two totally different human beings. There's a little bit of me and a little bit of Jen in both girls. At times it's quite frightening to witness because you know where their DNA comes from—straight from me and Momma.

I'm a girl dad through and through. I'm proud to be able to be the father I want to be for them. I'm not going to lie: I snap at them sometimes. But being a father has taught me a lot of patience, that's for damn sure.

Siena, our oldest, is hard-headed, willing to do whatever it takes on her own. Very independent. She has the will to get through whatever is in front of her. The first time I put skates on her, she did not want any help holding her up. For days on end she was falling down and getting up. She was going to do it by herself. That's the mentality she has.

And then there's Avery, the youngest, who couldn't give two shits about what other people are doing. She'll go and do her own thing every time. Avery is definitely not a follower. I feel Avery is more like me. I was the younger sibling who looked up to my brother. I reminisce and cherish the moments I had with my brother at that age. But I also remember my brother telling me to go away and leave him alone, to quit following him around. I see that with Siena and Avery—Siena saying, "My friends are here. You go play by yourself."

We want them to be free-spirited. I never had that growing

up. And we want them to have structure. I think that's what kids crave. I never had that. There was no structure in our home.

I am grateful that I am able to be here every day for them. I know how important a father is to their children. I'm not going to risk being absent. My retirement from hockey came at the perfect moment. I know a lot of my ex-teammates envy me being around my kids every day because they didn't have that. They were still playing. They weren't around their kids watching them grow up.

My daughters' lives will be very different than mine.

My parents have raised all four of my sister's kids. That's just the way of life up there. My sister's kids, like a lot of others, will be at their grandparents' house 24/7 from the day they are born until they're teenagers. I've asked Corinne how she can allow her kids to grow up in the same environment we grew up in. But you only know what you know. It's almost like a rule that every grandkid is going to be raised in their grandparents' home.

It was never going to be like that for my girls. I get random comments from my mom about it—"Oh, your girls are never going to know who we are." Mom, they know who you are. We talk about you guys all the time. But in her eyes, because they're not physically there for her to look after, she feels they're not going to know her. When we FaceTime with her, the kids will do it for a few minutes, but then they want to go off and play—because they're kids. "It's because they think I'm too ugly," my mom will say. "That's why they don't want to talk."

I've told her we are totally capable of raising our own kids in a healthy environment. And that she shouldn't be saying that shit.

I am also going to make sure that both Siena and Avery know what it is like to be out on the land. Both of our girls love the outdoors. I think one of the keys to having an open mind is being able to go outside and explore. That's one of the most important things for me: to make sure my girls know where I'm from and the experiences I've had. For me to take them up to the North and show them what it takes to be out on the land and how life is so freeing out there. They haven't really experienced Nunavut camping yet, being so young and because of the pandemic. But I guarantee you that when they do, they'll embrace it with open arms.

8 I Needed a Plan

After Lou left the Devils, Ray Shero became the new general manager in New Jersey. I had him in Nashville, so that transition was pretty smooth. And they changed the coaches, bringing in Geoff Ward.

Even with the uncertainty that comes with new coaches, not knowing how much I was going to play or what role they would put me in, I had a great second season in New Jersey. I wound up playing between ten and fifteen minutes a night and on the power play. It gave me new life. But after that season, they weren't interested in bringing me back.

At the end of the year, I was a free agent. I also had to have surgery on my wrist and was in a mini-cast.

I remember that I was in Dallas, at my buddy's wedding, three or four days after free agency opened when I got a call from Jonathan Toews, Brent Seabrook and Duncan Keith. It was a conference call, and Taser was saying, "Hey Toots, we'd really love to have you on our team. Would you be interested?"

"Fuck, yeah," I said.

The Blackhawks . . . a great team, and this would be a great opportunity for me to try to win a Stanley Cup. I was really honestly shocked. That meant a lot to me—that those players wanted me.

Their general manager, Stan Bowman, called me about a half-hour later. "Toots," he said, "I let my core guys pick our team, and they're really interested in you. Would you like to come to Chicago? I know you had a wrist surgery. We just need our doctor to clear you."

I flew from Dallas to Chicago and a courtesy car picked me up and drove me right to the team doctor's house. I rang the doorbell, and Dr. Terry answered.

"Take your brace off," he said. "I need to look at your wrist." He gave it a couple of twists and then said, "Welcome to the Chicago Blackhawks. I think you're good to go."

The truth is, my wrist was still in a lot of pain, because I had just had surgery . . . but that was it. It was a stress-free summer after that, knowing what I had to look forward to.

Chicago was an unbelievable experience. I couldn't have been happier playing for one of the best teams in the league—and wearing the best logo in all of professional sports. That logo carries a lot of pride and tradition and culture. Being Indigenous, it meant a lot to me.

I know some people don't like the logo. But I think all sports should have the Redskins, the Indians, the Eskimos. That's my opinion. I think it's a reflection on history. I don't understand why it has to come down to being a racial term.

There was a fantastic environment around the Blackhawks. I knew my role going into training camp: fourth line, in and out. I accepted it because that was part of my sacrifice in return for the opportunity to win a Cup. At that point in my career, I was comfortable and content with that fourth-line label. I just showed up every day, whether I was in the lineup or not. I fucking put my head down and battled.

Joel Quenneville is a straight-up coach. That's all any player wants: someone who is honest, who puts all the bullshit aside. Just tell me if I'm in or not. Don't send me home after three games saying, "We've got to see because we've got a couple of injured guys." Fucking just tell me now. Q was like that.

"Toots, you're in the lineup. Be ready," he'd say.

That's all I needed to hear.

I loved playing in the United Center. It's the loudest building in the NHL. I played there for twelve years on the visitors' bench, listening to the anthem and having chills go down my spine. Imagine playing every night at home in front of that crowd and listening to that anthem. It was spectacular.

I was thinking that whatever happened, if this was going to be my last year, I'd make the best of it.

In February 2017, Stan Bowman called me into his office. The Vegas Golden Knights were joining the NHL the next year, and an expansion draft was coming up in the spring. The 'Hawks wanted to protect some of their guys. "We need to sign another veteran," he told me. "Would you be willing to sign again?"

"Fuck, yeah," I thought. "I'll take another 750 grand guaranteed. It doesn't matter where I end up. I'll make it work."

And so I signed.

The 'Hawks finished first in the West and we played Nashville in the first round of the playoffs that year. I got into two games. Something I said during that series got kind of blown out of proportion by the media. The quote was along the lines of "It's great to be on this side of the bench with the opportunity that we have," and the Nashville media fucking exploded. They spun it as though I was saying that when I played for the Preds, we didn't have a great chance to win, and now that I was with Chicago, we did. There was quite a bit of backlash.

In the end, we lost that series, and our season was over.

I still had another year on my contract, but I was thinking, "Whatever happens happens." If I got picked up in the expansion draft, fine. If I got put on waivers, I was good with it. And if it came down to it, I would also be good with just being done.

I didn't get picked in the expansion draft. So, I reported to training camp with Chicago in September and I thought things were looking good. And then, a day before the final roster was set, Stan Bowman called me in.

"Toots, we're going to put you on waivers," he said. "Unfortunately, you're the odd man out."

By that time, I was actually okay if I didn't get picked up by another team. I knew deep in my heart that I wasn't willing to battle it out in the minors to try and get back into the NHL.

When I wasn't claimed by anyone, I went in to talk to Stan.

"Hey look," I said, "I did you guys a favour by signing, because you were stuck as far as signing another veteran guy. Now, it's your turn to return the favour. I'm not going down to Rockford [their AHL affiliate]. My wife's pregnant, she's due in February. I'm not moving back and forth with my daughter and my wife. Put me on long-term injured reserve, and do whatever you have to in order to make it look right, because I'm not going to go play in Rockford—end of story."

My shoulder really had been bugging me quite a bit. Stan said, "Get me an MRI on the shoulder and we'll use that as our out."

And so that's what happened. I packed my bags and went down to Rockford for one pre-game skate just to say that I was there and that I wasn't ready to play, healthwise. Then I went on long-term IR and never heard from anybody in the organization for the rest of the year.

I knew that was probably the end of my playing career, and I accepted it. I made the best of being home every day with the family, so I had something to look forward to away from the game. I didn't miss playing. I didn't miss being on the ice every day. I was actually comfortable with it, and there was no pressure coming from anywhere to try and get me back into hockey.

I did get some offers from European teams throughout the summer and into the fall, and I thought about taking the opportunity to play overseas. If I was going to play in Europe, I wanted to play in a great city in a great location—preferably in Switzerland, where the travel is short and they play mostly on weekends, or in Italy, where Jen's family is from. I was still healthy. I took care of myself. I just didn't want to play at a high level anymore—I wanted to find a country club, where there was no pressure and I could just show up and enjoy the game.

A few European teams offered me contracts. But ultimately, my decision came down to my family, having two young kids. Although it would have been the perfect situation to take the kids away before they were in school, I just felt like there were too many moving parts.

Plus, I realized I was kind of over the game. I was fucking done.

A lot of hockey players have trouble adjusting to retirement. The biggest reason that I didn't was that I had met Mike Watson.

I had been introduced to him through my agent. I admit that when I met with Watty the first time, I thought, "Fuck, why am I doing this?" It was the spring after I got out of rehab and was back playing with the Predators. I figured I was going to play hockey there for the next ten years. So, why would I need to start doing this now? Why the fuck was my agent hooking me up with this guy?

Mike rented a boardroom in one of the hotels and I went down one afternoon after practice to meet him. We sat in that room with a whiteboard for four or five hours. He stood up there and we wrote down pages and pages of shit, and that's how it started: creating my own brand and talking about what my visions and goals were. I had never done that before in my life.

It was quite interesting, to say the least. I didn't know what it was going to lead to. But working with Mike and helping him find what I enjoy, what interests me, really made my transition into life after hockey a lot smoother. Of course, because of my background, I'm a bit of a unique story compared to a lot of professional athletes.

Retirement is not an easy transition for players. There are a lot of retired guys who live near me in Kelowna, and I remember being in the gym with one of them. It was his first year out of the game. I was already retired and out doing speaking engagements.

The player told me he was still working out every day, but that he didn't have any sense of purpose after retiring. "Why can't I do what you're doing, Toots?" The thing is, I didn't wake up the day after my retirement and announce, "Hey, I'm going to be a public speaker." I started branding myself eight years before that. But when you're a 23-year-old hockey player, all you're thinking about is the game. You think you can do that for the rest of your life. Then, *boom*, you get a career-ending injury or you get cut and you're out of the league. Now what? You don't know who you are. You don't know what interests you. You don't know your brand. All you know is hockey.

Hockey has given me everything. I owe my life to the game because of all of the opportunities it provided. If I had stayed in Rankin and been a Joe Schmoe, I would never have been able to share my story with the public. But even with hockey and playing in the NHL, I needed a plan. And I've got Watty to thank for that.

And I know Mike won't mind me sharing that he has gone through his own battle for sobriety. When I first connected with him, he would smell like booze every morning when I met with him. To be honest, there was a little bit of worry for me there. Watty was into going out and entertaining—and Nashville is the entertainment capital of the world. We stuck it out, and eventually I helped Watty get over that hump. It ain't fucking easy, man.

When you're in the corporate world, you go to these conferences that turn into big piss-ups. I've been on speaking engagements with corporate groups, and I have no problem calling people out. Not individually, but sometimes I look at those faces and I can see myself coming to practice on the morning after. You want to hang out in the weeds and hope nobody notices you. That was me in the dressing room or hiding in the players' lounge with a coffee and trying not to be seen by anyone.

Half the corporate guys who come to hear me talk about how I got sober are probably fucking hungover and hating their lives—and I tell them that. There is always laughter when I say it, but I also see a lot of heads go down—because they know.

9 You've Got to Take Those Painful Emotions Head-on

I decided to officially announce my retirement from hockey in the fall of 2018. And I decided that the place I had to do it was Brandon, Manitoba: the place where I established myself in junior hockey, and the place where my brother died.

By going back to Brandon, I thought I could mentally close that chapter of my life on a high note, and close the door on the trauma that city had caused for me and my family. I went through a lot there, and I had a lot of time to reflect on it. I felt it was my duty to go back and celebrate hockey and the city and what it had given me when I was playing for the Wheat Kings. And by going back, I could also keep Terence's name and legend alive. He did so much for me, and now I had a chance to reflect and talk about what he taught me even in our last moments together, while laying everything else to rest.

I hadn't been drinking for years, and I was in a very different headspace. I would have all of my family there and it would be an opportunity for all of us to celebrate my hockey career and to celebrate my brother's life.

It would also be a great opportunity for Jennifer to go back and close a few chapters in her own life. When I first talked to Jen about it, her eyes glowed and she said she thought it was a chance for us as a family, a chance for our kids, to see where I started my career, where we met, and to do some healing.

I knew that coming back to Brandon would be hard for my parents, having to face the public and realizing that everyone knew what had happened to Terence there.

But you've got to take those painful emotions head-on.

You probably already know the story.

It was August 2002. I was getting ready for what would be my last season of junior, playing for the Wheat Kings, after being drafted by Nashville in 2001.

As a nineteen-year-old kid, it was pretty tough to digest the whole situation immediately. Terence and I were out partying with some friends that night, the same way we had thousands of times before. In a few days he was going to be flying to the States to try out for the Norfolk Admirals in the American Hockey League. We were all drinking. Terence was driving. I tried to talk him into staying over at my girlfriend's house, but he wanted to drive back to our billet house on the edge of town.

I found out later that the Brandon cops pulled him over right after he dropped us off. He blew over the limit, but instead of them taking him to the station the way they were supposed to with people who are intoxicated, they took him to Neil and Janine Roy's place, where we lived. They knew who he was. Everyone in town knew who we were.

We found Terence the next night, in a field near the house. He had taken the shotgun that we used for hunting.

He left me a note:

Jor, go all the way. Take care of the family. You are the man. Terence.

Terence's death obviously had a huge impact on my family. For a good year or two after that, a lot of family members slowed down their addictions or substance abuse issues. But within my immediate family, there was so much grieving going on, and a lot of silent treatment. Did my parents ever look back and reflect and say, "Hey, were we the root cause of all this?" Or were they stuck in their old ways and blaming the system?

For a long time I just couldn't understand what had happened that night. All I knew was that Terence was living his best life at that time. How could somebody take their own life when they've got the world in their hands? His dream was to play pro hockey and it was right at his fingertips.

It's hard for me to put what happened to my brother into a few sentences. All of the bad experiences that he lived through . . .

Terence was everything to me, a guy to lean on. He was the guy who was a parent to our parents. He was the guy who took me to school and picked me up from school, took me to hockey practice—and he was only fucking sixteen, seventeen years old at the time. He was so mentally tough. How could that guy kill himself?

For a long time I just couldn't put two and two together as to why an individual in his situation would take their own life at that moment. I was like a lot of people who lose a loved one and don't know the whole story. It takes time for everything to start coming together.

I blamed myself because I was with him that evening. I often thought maybe if we hadn't gone out, he wouldn't have killed himself and he'd still be here today. I was also looking for someone else to blame. The Brandon police, those fucking cocksuckers, didn't do their job. I wasn't even looking at my parents. Who in their right mind would blame the people they love the most? But you don't know until you start looking at it differently.

As time went on and I was digging into the history of us growing up, I started to come to the realization that there was a lot more to Terence's suicide than our actions that night. It took time for me to realize that it wasn't all the Brandon police's fault, to stop thinking that it wouldn't have happened if they had just taken him down to the station.

In rehab there was a lot of self-reflection and putting pen to paper, trying to go back to all the incidents I could remember within our family home. They started to pile up. There were hundreds of times when Terence was called upon to mediate the family or look after Dad when he was all pissed up. Looking at the damage it did to my brother, I don't know how he did it.

Slowly, slowly, I started to think, "Hey, maybe it wasn't my fault." There was a lot more weighing on his shoulders than that one night we went out and he got pulled over. We'd been pulled over before and got off. You would think that would be a red flag to not drink and drive. But when you think you're invincible and everyone counts on you to get from point A to point B, it doesn't matter if you have twenty beers in you. A lot of us counted on Terence on nights like that because he was always the one who pulled through, just like he was the one who would put his head down when he was getting a tap on the shoulder from my mom at three, four in the morning to go pick up Dad. There was never a question. He just did it.

But in the months and years that followed Terence's death, I tried to block out those bad memories with booze and the game of hockey. I went to my first training camp with Nashville that fall, and then came back to play with the Wheat Kings. Our schedule was pretty busy every day during the season. It was during the off-season that the mental and emotional and physical stress were the worst, when I was home all day, not having my brother around.

Those first couple of summers after Terence died, I was living in Winnipeg. My uncle Luc was there and my auntie Dorothy. It was an easy place for me to jump on a plane and go home to Rankin Inlet whenever I wanted to, plus a lot of Inuit come down to the city, so I was able to see a lot of familiar faces.

It helped me pass those evenings being with somebody. Somebody to use, somebody to drink with. It was more of a comfort thing. I knew I wasn't going to be home alone all night, so I would drink myself to bed with my visitors.

Booze was everything to me at that time. It helped me loosen up. I thought it created the masculine side of me. I thought that extra confidence after having a few drinks would show everybody that I was doing fine, even though I had lost my brother.

I'm sure there were people who looked at me and said, "Well, he's on the path to destruction, but I'm going to stay clear of him because he's playing in the NHL and he's doing what he loves to do." I know for a fact there were a lot of relatives and family members who were concerned but just didn't have the balls to tell me straight up. They didn't want to ruin their relationship with me because I was playing in the NHL. "Let's just keep Jordin happy," they were thinking.

Everyone wanted to be around me, and I thought that brought me happiness. But no one had the fucking balls to tell me the truth. There was never anyone who would say no to me—and I used that as a tool.

All addicts find a way to convince people that everything's good and that if you just stick around with them, they'll look after you. I kind of groomed them, whether it was forcing them to drink with me or forcing them to stay up all night with me because I was a selfish fuck.

I was drinking a lot more than ever. I'd go on benders. I was still functional enough to do my off-season workouts, but the rest of the day I would belly up to a restaurant at lunchtime and have a few beers and then have a barbecue in the evening and a couple more bottles of wine.

I masked a lot of my feelings for the first four or five years after Terence passed away. I had the game of hockey to keep me busy, to keep my mind off of my personal life. The spotlight was on me in making the NHL, which made it easier to sweep that whole situation under the rug. Then, when I would come home to Nunavut, it was a two-week piss-up where I just never had time to fucking sit down and talk about what had happened.

The truth is, I had no clue how to do that, to actually talk about life. I didn't have the courage because I knew what my parents were capable of—and they were still using.

I didn't really start to understand what had happened to Terence until I had clarity in my own life. I really started connecting a lot of dots when I went to rehab. I was writing my individual timeline as a kid growing up, going through each year and trying to remember all the incidents that happened, all of the physical and mental abuse. I never, ever thought about that when I was using because I would drink to forget about everything. I didn't want to deal with that emotional roller-coaster ride because I was already dealing with my hockey career and my family and people that were close to me, and I thought that brought me comfort and peace. But in actuality it created more stress.

Not drinking is hard. You have to create a new life in adulthood, finding new hobbies, finding new friends. When you become sober, you've got to listen to your body and find new avenues to happiness. Relapse usually happens because in sobriety it's too hard to handle all of the emotions. You think, "I might as well go back to drinking because it was a lot easier." It's very difficult, especially when you live in a remote community, to find a new life in sobriety when everyone else around you is using, especially your tight group of friends.

One of the first things I did when I went home to Rankin after rehab was to tell all of my childhood friends that I didn't want them to feel uncomfortable when I was around because I chose not to drink. They all used to see my coming home as the chance for a big piss-up. That was just the way it was in the North. It eased some pressure with my buddies when I told them I didn't give a shit what they decided to do—drink or not—when I was around. That was their issue. I didn't want them to feel like they couldn't be themselves around me because I wasn't drinking.

After I moved from Winnipeg to Kelowna as my off-season home, I did a lot of work with a therapist there. Before that, I hid a lot from therapists because I didn't want to relive those situations. I thought I had finished with that during my thirty days in rehab. It turned out that that was just the tip of the iceberg. It wasn't until three or four years into sobriety that I started to really dig deep down and ask my parents some questions. But it was almost like they were embarrassed to relive the events because they knew what they had put us through.

I finally started to come to terms with our childhood and what we experienced, and how that might have affected Terence's decision to take his own life. I'm not going to say I wasn't a part of the last night. I was there. When I would digest the whole thing, I was only looking at the last three days we spent together and it was the best time of his life. How the fuck could this happen? But I started to understand that it was about everything prior to those last three days. And I started to understand that he wasn't the only one.

Before Terence's passing I would hear about one or two or three suicides a year within the community in Rankin Inlet. As a kid, I didn't quite understand. There was a girl who was in my class when I was eleven, twelve years old and she took her own life. I remember thinking, "What the hell? I was just at school with her yesterday." That was the one that really stood out to me as a kid growing up. Suicide wasn't really as much of a topic of conversation in the community in those days. Maybe there were a lot of suicides, but there wasn't social media back then. It wasn't publicized.

Now it feels like almost every other day someone's taking their own life, and maybe it's more prevalent because people can't come to terms with owning their experiences. People are afraid to carry that shame. As soon as they tell their story, or when they speak to someone about it, it's hard for them to live in the community where everyone knows everyone. So they revert to suicide. They think it's easier to not face other people.

I grew up in a house where nothing was ever talked about, so we were able to function without people knowing our fucking dirt. Now everything's out there, which is better, but we've got to be able to have the coping skills to overcome the shame and the guilt. We all have our dark secrets. We all fight a fight that no one knows about until we open up and become one as a community.

But the thing that pisses me off is that the community only comes together when there's a death or a tragedy. We need to celebrate individuals in our communities and uplift them while they are alive.

I know my mom is still grieving for Terence to this day. Two or three years after losing him, she started having a lot of mental health issues. She's the one who's struggling the most. She keeps my brother's ashes in an urn in her bedroom. I'd walk in there and see it and think, "I wish we could let go as a family." But my mom says, "You don't know how much I fucking miss him. You don't know how I'm dealing with it every day." Every time she walks into her room, she looks at that urn. You're never going to forget about it, but for your own mental sake, you need to move forward in life.

I couldn't imagine, as a parent, what it must be like losing a kid. But man, living for twenty years in mental distress . . .

I look back at my childhood and what I experienced then. Having clarity about it really helps me deal with those inner feelings and doubts about Terence's death, wondering what I could have done differently. Why did we have to go out that night? Why didn't I stay with him?

All those questions—I finally let go.

10 You Have Better in You

I called Kelly McCrimmon, who was the general manager of the Wheat Kings when I played there and still one of the owners of the team, and asked him if they'd be willing to host my retirement press conference. Crimm had the office staff reach out to me and it just kind of snowballed. We picked a date that made sense, a Saturday night when the Wheat Kings were playing at home.

It has taken years for it to really sink in how much Crimm cared for me as a person, and how much I put him through over the years. I don't know how one guy could put up with so much bullshit—not just verbal bullshit, but my actions.

When I got drafted by the Wheat Kings, I didn't really know what the Western Hockey League was all about. Someone from the team called me to congratulate me, and honestly I didn't quite understand the whole process. Everyone was talking about this kid from Nunavut getting drafted into the WHL. I'm still not sure how the hell I even got noticed.

They had a few scouts who travelled around. One of them was a gentleman by the name of Rick Knickle who was a goalie back in his day. He was an ex-pro and had played his junior hockey in Brandon. I think he saw me play one game in The Pas and suggested to Kelly that they take me.

I had a lengthy phone chat with Kelly about what to expect. I hadn't even met the guy in person yet, but I felt like he was true to his word. In the hockey world, the *political* hockey world, you have coaches and GMs bullshitting players all the time. But I really sensed that Kelly was sincere with me, even though I didn't know a lot about him.

When I met Kelly, I felt an instant connection with him. The first time we talked faced to face, I told him a bit about my life. In those days I shielded a lot of my personal demons because I had a lot of baggage. That wasn't just me. It was the same for any player back then—the less you said, the better off you were. You didn't want to be labelled as a problem child or a cancer in the dressing room. You can be the best hockey player in the world, but if you are open about off-ice issues, it could damage your career.

But I felt that deep inside Crimmer somehow knew my story right off the bat. The connection between us was almost instant. He became like a father figure. He really cared about Jordin Tootoo the person, not just the hockey player. I always felt safe around him.

At that age, I also started to realize that there was a lot of politics in the hockey world. That wasn't the way I grew up. The way I was brought up, things were black and white—tell me what I need to work on to get better. Don't sugar-coat anything or make promises. I just had it in my DNA to show up and go to work. On the ice I always felt that if I did my job, it would trump everything off the ice. But it wasn't really that simple.

When I showed up in Brandon as a sixteen-year-old, I was a scared teenager about to be on my own for the first time after playing with my brother on the OCN team in The Pas the year before. (The Opaskwayak Cree Nation in northern Manitoba have a team in the Manitoba Junior Hockey League—one level below major junior hockey.)

Looking back, I think Crimm must have known about my family dynamic somehow—maybe from talking to some of my relatives or friends who would come down for games. But in those days I always felt like I was being attacked every time I was called into his office. My guard was always up. He was always the one who was the hardest on me, but at the end of the conversation, he would always say, "I'm here for you." I guess that was tough love.

Halfway through my rookie season, I still didn't know my limits. I had already played in The Pas with a bunch of nineteen- and twenty-year-olds who loved to have a good time. And we won a lot, so it didn't seem to affect our performance on the ice. But in the WHL, it was no cakewalk anymore. You were under a pretty strict set of rules. Did I abide by all the rules? No. That's why I was called into the office quite a bit.

There are a couple of incidents with Kelly that I remember really well.

One happened in the middle of my last year in junior. The Tragically Hip were in town on a Saturday night and we had the weekend off. We all got tickets to the concert. Sunday, we had practice at 10 a.m. Well, I'm the fucking stud of the team, right? I'm fucking cocky. Fucking green light, boys, let's go. Tragically Hip. Party all night.

I woke up at noon the next day. Oh shit, my phone . . . It's my fucking agent. I missed practice. McCrimmon had left a message and he's yelling, "Where the fuck are you? Get your fucking ass down here." Oh shit.

As soon as I got to the rink, I walked into his office. He got up and slammed the door behind me. "Sit the fuck down, Toots," he said. "You're fucking done. You're fucking done. I'm cutting you from the team. I'm sending you home. That's it."

"Fuck you, McCrimmon," I yelled back. "Trade me."

I was still fucking half-cut, hungover, and I was thinking, "I'm not taking no shit from you like I did from my dad."

"Trade me right fucking now."

I got up, walked out, slammed the door.

Kelly chased me down.

"You're done," he said. "Don't come to the fucking rink for two weeks."

"Yeah, no problem," I said.

I was acting all tough. Then I got in my car, and I remember thinking, "What the fuck just happened?" It was like I snapped out of it. "How am I going to explain this to my mom? How am I going to explain this to everyone?"

I couldn't really go anywhere, so I locked myself in my billets' basement for a few days because of the shame and guilt. I understood the message Kelly was trying to send: I don't give a shit if you're a star player. These are the team rules.

I can't fully recall all the details about the other incident with Crimm now, but I know it was a time when I felt broken. I was in his office, meeting with him, and it was the first time I ever bawled in front of another human being.

Kelly started tearing up as well. "I just want you to let me in," he said. "I'm here for you. Anything you need."

I think that was one of the first moments where I kind of broke down and realized that someone cared about me as a person, not just as a fucking hockey player. Kelly tried to take me under his wing. After I was drafted, he helped me get ready for the NHL and my first training camp. He had dealt with a lot of guys who had gone on to play pro.

Kelly was the one who drove me to Winnipeg to meet my mom and dad the day my brother died and tell them what had happened.

I left the Wheat Kings on a sour note. The passing of my brother. The constant getting in shit. I just felt like, "Fuck, I need to get out of here." When I went to the Nashville Predators' training camp as a twenty-year-old, I didn't know if I was going to make the team, but the last thing I wanted was to wind up back in Brandon for another year of junior. So I fucking busted my ass off and sacrificed. I moved to Nashville at the beginning of August to start training and to get away from all of the fuck-ing bullshit and partying. It all worked out. It was a long fuck-ing month, being by myself in the hotel and craving drinks on a nightly basis (you had to be twenty-one to drink in the bars there). I had to hold back some major inner demons. I was lonely until the last week, when I was able to get my best friend, Troy, down from Nunavut to spend time with me and push me through the last part of training until camp started.

I had phone calls from Crimmer throughout that month. I guess he had the inside scoop from the Predators' coach, Barry Trotz, and the general manager, David Poile. He encouraged me to stick with it because he knew I had a great opportunity to make the team. That's the kind of belief that he had in me. Think about all of the stress I had put him through, and he was still willing to reach out to me. At the time, I took it for granted. I was actually fed up with hearing from him all the time. Every time I'd see his number come up on the phone, I'd think, "Fuck, what am I going to get in shit for now?" But when I look back, I realize how much he had invested in me.

I think there was a lot of communication over the years between Crimm and the people in Nashville. "How do we deal with Toots? What are his issues?" But that was all behind the scenes.

Maybe that's why Trotsy treated me like I was his son. He'd call me into his office and the first thing I'd be thinking was, "What the fuck did I do now?"—the same way I did with Kelly. But I realize now that, just like Crimm, he was looking out for me.

———

Before my retirement announcement, the last time I had been in Brandon was in 2010. The city was hosting the Memorial Cup that year and it was basically a piss-up for me. To be honest, I really don't remember much about that whole weekend. I just felt numb. Being in a selfish state of mind at that point, I didn't really want to spend too much time sitting in a quiet space by myself because I just didn't want to deal with those emotions. So, I kept busy by roaming around the city, going to old friends' places, having a beer here, having a beer there. When I was in the pub at the arena, I felt like there was a guard around me and that I was invincible. But that's because I was under the influence. I always would use "liquid courage" to shield myself from what I was really thinking. That was the year before I went into rehab.

Kelly called me into his office, just like old times, except that by then I'd been playing in The Show.

I sat down and cracked a beer right on his fucking desk.

He looked at me, shook his head, and said, "Still doing that shit, hey Toots?"

Fuck, here we go. But now I'm a grown man.

"You can give me all the shit you want," I said, "but I don't have to take it anymore."

That's when he said, "Toots, I believe in you. You have better in you." And I was thinking, "Why are you talking to me like that?" I couldn't accept his heart-to-heart.

"You can turn your life around," he said. "I'm here for you."

When the tournament was over, I kind of Houdini'd. I disappeared right after the championship game. I remember saying to a couple of my buddies, "Let's just get out of town. I don't want to face the reality of this being sober."

After that, Crimmer and I still had that love-hate relationship. I still felt like he was always on my back. I didn't really understand until I got into sobriety that it was his way of saying he cared about me.

I can reflect now on those certain moments and realize that I had never had that before from anyone. And he allowed my culture, my people, to come into the arena and into the dressing room and share the triumphs.

11 We Can Only Keep Going

Flying into Winnipeg on the way to Brandon the day before the retirement press conference, the reality of it hit me as soon as I landed at the airport. I've always internalized my feelings and my thoughts. But now I had to face them—and face them sober.

When we got to our hotel room in Brandon, I just lay there on the couch. My two little girls were playing on the floor, and I shed a few tears because the emotions were going through me, and I couldn't hold them back. I think it was an opportunity for me to let go.

It was a stressful few days because I was trying to keep everyone happy, like I always used to, and especially making sure my parents, my sister and her family were all looked after. But I was also in high demand. I was so busy doing interviews and going places that I couldn't really home in on talking about the whole situation with my mom and dad.

I hoped it was going to be an opportunity for my parents to stop playing the blame game. To this day, they still blame people in Brandon for what happened to Terence. I couldn't imagine what it was like for them to lose a child and have to go back to where it all happened. But I think and hope it was a milestone in their lives, a chance to heal a little bit. To have comfort.

When I told my mom what I was planning to do, her first reaction was: "I don't think I have the courage to go back there." I kind of coaxed her into making the trip. I told her it was okay to let go and to release whatever she was feeling. It was a chance to move forward as a family, a great opportunity for all of us to celebrate my brother and just be together.

My sister, Corinne, is kind of like my father. She's very quiet and never really talks much. There were times in Brandon where we were sitting by ourselves and reflecting on Terence's life and shedding a few tears together. I think that was really the only time my sister and I had an opportunity to do that. When we were at home in Rankin Inlet, there were people around all the time. When it was just me and her in my hotel room, I think it really sank in for her that our family was back together, fifteen years later. It was a chance for her to kind of let go, and I felt that she really got to that point.

I remember her telling me, "You know, there's nothing that we can do about what happened. We can only keep going." Those were pretty strong words to come out of my sister's mouth.

———

One of the things I wanted to do in Brandon was sit down with my old billets, Neil and Janine Roy. They were the best thing that happened to me during my hockey career in Brandon.

When you play junior hockey, the team sets you up with a billet family. They are paid to provide you with room and board and a home environment. For sixteen-year-olds arriving in a strange town, most of them living independently for the first time, getting the right billet is incredibly important.

The first billet house where I lived in Brandon was a disaster. I felt like I was of no value to their family as a human being. I was like an outsider looking in.

I remember saying to Kelly, "Fuck, I can't live here anymore. They don't understand me."

"Toots," he said, "we're trying." It was a long time before I realized he actually meant it.

Then he found Terence and me a place with Neil and Janine.

I consider them and their three boys to be family. If it weren't for them bringing me into their home, I don't think I ever would've gotten through that stage of my life. They gave me support and understanding. They took in our culture, our family dynamics, the way that we grew up and my parents' mindset—they took all of that into consideration. I was welcomed into their home with open arms and I felt no judgment from them. It was like a clean slate for me after two years of living with my prior billets, where I just felt like I was in the way. The Roys dove right in and allowed me to eat my traditional foods and have my family and friends stay there. I looked at them almost as parents.

Our communication was kind of cut off when I left Brandon. I don't know if there was anger in me, or if it was sadness or if I was trying to blame somebody else for Terence's death. When I left Brandon, I wanted to forget about everything that had happened, so I distanced myself from a lot of people, and they didn't deserve that. We kept in contact, but it was very superficial stuff—nothing more than "Hey, how are you doing?"

They still live in the same place where Terence died. I wanted to go out to their farm, but I didn't want to cause any drama. With my parents being there, I just wanted to keep everyone happy. The last thing I wanted to do was ask my parents, "Do you want to go out to Neil and Janine's and say our last goodbyes?"

I know for a fact that there had been a barrier there, and I know they felt terrible about what happened on their property. I couldn't imagine what they'd had going through their minds over the last twenty years.

I know that my parents directed a lot of blame towards them—like it was all their fault. There was a lot of tension between my parents and them for many years.

Neil and Janine were a very touchy subject in my family. I was a little nervous when everyone was going to be in the same room in Brandon. Was something going to happen? Was my mom going to blow up at them? We got together at the hotel and I think it was good for all of us—especially for Janine, who had been battling cancer for a number of years. When I saw them, I gave them a big hug and thanked them. A lot of weight lifted off my shoulders, and I hope off theirs, too.

Thankfully, everything was cordial and everything went smoothly when they saw my parents. I feel like my mom finally let that grudge go.

The press conference to officially announce my retirement was in the arena in the afternoon. There was a game there that night. I was in our hotel room, getting ready for the announcement, when my mother asked me if she could read my speech.

"Well, no," I said. "I'm still working on it."

Mom wanted to know beforehand what I was going to say, if I was going to expose her and my dad, if it was going to reflect badly on them.

"I want everyone to hear it from my mouth for the first time," I told her.

At least it wasn't a fight, which was a change because with our history, it was always a fight.

Being in the Keystone Centre, walking those hallways that I walked in for five years, brought back a lot of great memories. Even the smell of the barn brought me back to my teenage years playing for the Wheat Kings. The room where we held the press conference was the exact same room where I used to do homework for two hours after every practice. Looking around at the walls, I was remembering how much I used to hate being there.

But this time when I walked into that room, I enjoyed every minute of it.

I tried to block out all of the emotions when I started my speech, but then it all just started coming through me. Seeing my two little girls and my family in the audience, it was kind of a reality check. "Wow, I'm a grown-ass man now. I have my own family." I had to be strong for them, yet show that vulnerability, show that it's okay to talk about the hard times and the experiences and shed a few tears. My family was going to see me crying in public, which they had never really experienced before. I knew that if I shed tears, they were really tears of joy.

My mind was racing. I just wanted to really talk from my heart—and I did.

Thank you all for being here. This is a pretty special day for me and my family.

I appreciate you taking the time to share this day with us. I decided to read some formal remarks to you. This is a big day for my family and I want to get it right.

After four years in the WHL and fifteen years in the NHL, it is time for me to retire from the NHL.

It is pretty special being back here in Brandon. It is a symbolic statement about something that has come full circle. When I came to Brandon all those years ago, I didn't think much of the role I needed to play as a role model for my people. I was just a hockey player that would fight with everything I had to make the NHL.

This community embraced me and looked beyond my background and just judged me for how I played the game.

Thank you, Rick Dillabough, Grant Armstrong, the entire Brandon Wheat Kings organization, and especially Mr. McCrimmon for allowing my family and me to be here today. And thank you to the people of Brandon, who embraced my brother and me.

I have been blessed with a four-year WHL career and a fifteen-year NHL career.

I want to thank all of the NHL organizations whose jerseys I had the honour of wearing. Chicago, New Jersey, Detroit and, of course, Nashville. It is difficult to describe the emotion I feel as I look back. I will sum it up in one word: gratitude.

The camaraderie with the players and the connection with the fans is something you need to experience to believe. It has enriched my life beyond words.

I owe my life to this game. The city of Nashville embraced me when I arrived as a youngster grieving the loss of his big brother. It was David Poile and Barry Trotz who helped me realize I needed help with my alcoholism, it was Ken Holland who believed in me when I was early in my recovery, Lou Lamoriello who brought me in and trusted me when it looked like my legs might be slowing, and Stan Bowman who showed nothing but class in my final year. Gentlemen, you are class acts. And I thank you.

To my teammates, both when life was a little haywire and when life settled down, thank you. You have given me memories and bonds that I will cherish for a lifetime.

And, to the fans. It is you who make it so much fun. Playing in front of you for almost twenty years has been an incredible honour.

And, to my parents and my sister. Mom, Dad and Corinne, you gave me all you had to give. I cherish you.

Most of all, to my wife, Jen, and to my girls, Siena and Avery, thank you. You have helped me see the real meaning of life. And you are my life.

I am retiring with no regrets. It has been a great run and now it is time for the next chapter.

I know I will always remain close to my Native roots and will continue to work to enhance life for Native children who are suffering. I am deeply concerned about some of the challenges facing our Indigenous population, especially teen suicide and untreated mental health challenges. I want to work with communities to create awareness around mental health and to support suicide prevention initiatives. This is a national problem. I want to speak to corporate Canada about creating a culture of inspired inclusivity. It's so important for companies today to build better teams where everyone feels welcome and is accepted.

I will leave this game at peace with myself, with the love of my family, and with memories that will last a lifetime.

The people of Rankin Inlet will understand this next comment. My brother, Terence, was my inspiration. Both in life and in the afterlife.

His final words to me were, "Jor, go all the way. Take care of the family. You are the man." I can only hope that I lived up to your expectations.

And, after fifteen years, it is time for me to retire from the NHL.

Thank you all. It's been one helluva ride.

In the middle of my speech, our eldest daughter, Siena, said loudly enough that everyone could hear: "Are you done yet, Ataata?" Everybody laughed. It kind of lightened that whole room, and I think that's when the joy really came through. Because of my kids and my wife and my family, I'm able to be who I want to be—to stop one cycle and start a new one.

I thought, "Okay, from here on in, it's time to celebrate my career and to celebrate my brother's life and leave Brandon on a positive note, knowing that whenever I go back, there's not going to be this cloud over me."

I got through that speech, and after that I could sense a lot of happiness within my family. This big moment was gone, we passed it, and now it was on to the next stage.

At the Wheat Kings' game later that night, they set up a table so that I could sign autographs during the first intermission.

It brought back a lot of memories. I recognized a few people who were kids when I was playing, and now they were grown adults. I was thinking, "Wow, throughout these years, they still remember who I am." I was always told by my father to sign every autograph for every kid. That's been my mantra since day one. You might have an hour pencilled in for meeting and greeting—but if it takes two hours to get through, it takes two hours. I'm going to make sure I meet everybody. No questions asked. That night, I didn't care if the game was going on or whatever. It was my opportunity to say thank you.

I remember when I was that little kid and athletes or other kinds of celebrities would come up to Rankin Inlet. I'd wait for that moment to actually meet a hero. It brings back a lot of great memories for me to see a young kid get all excited. Those are moments they will remember for the rest of their lives.

The fans told me old stories about certain games that they watched and remembered. It was very uplifting. They had put in their time and their money, buying tickets to come to the games, and now this was their time to spend with me. I felt a true heart-to-heart connection. And I really felt that there was a sense of peace amongst everybody there.

I've gone to a lot of First Nations communities where it's been chaos when I made a public appearance. That night in Brandon, because of my calmness, my demeanour, everyone just stayed cool and collected throughout the whole process. The people were waiting patiently in line, there was no barging, and I felt respected. If you respect me, that shows love and support, and ultimately that's what everyone demands—to feel loved—and I felt that in that moment.

There are a lot of reserves around Brandon. A lot of the young kids who came out were from there. They were too young to have watched me play, but their parents had. Those parents were showing their kids that it doesn't matter where you come from, or being Native—anything's possible because look, Jordin Tootoo did it. A lot of those really young kids were excited to meet me and to talk to me and get my autograph and a picture, even though they had only seen me play through YouTube videos. It felt like one big family gathering.

I think seeing that lineup of people put into perspective how much I meant to Brandon and the surrounding communities. When I was playing, I don't think I realized that. When you're in the middle of it, sometimes you create this bubble and you don't really see outside.

By the time I was finished signing autographs, the game was into the third period. That's how many people were there. I must have signed for every person in the arena—some of them more than once.

After the game, we went out for dinner at the hotel. I invited a lot of my buddies and people that I knew from town. We talked about the happy times, the good times, the bad times.

But there was one thing that was kind of hanging over me. My dad was having a few beers, so I knew by midnight it was time for me to head up to my room because I didn't want to be around him and alcohol. Who could tell what might happen? I just didn't want to be a part of it and ruin my celebration.

My father knows that I'm uncomfortable when he's drinking and that I don't want to be there. But you can't control what other people say or do. You can only control what you can control. I finally realized that in sobriety.

A lot of people came and said congratulations and a lot of stories were told. But I knew I had to lead by example. In the old days I was always the last one at the party. When I ducked out early, I'm sure a lot of my buddies were thinking, "This is not the Jordin we used to know back in his heyday. This guy's a changed man."

They were right.

The next morning—the one morning I wanted to have breakfast with my family—they were struggling to get out of bed. It wasn't early; it was nine o'clock. But they had all stayed out partying until two, three, four in the morning. It got to the point where I thought, "Fuck it. If you're down here, you're down here, and if you're not, I don't give a flying fuck." That's your decision, and if you don't respect me enough to come down and say one last goodbye at breakfast, if that's too much to ask, then you're irrelevant to me. I'll see you on the flip side.

But obviously that whole weekend had been an emotional roller-coaster ride and the last thing I wanted to do was leave on a bad note with everyone.

By the time they finally showed up, they were obviously foggy and not in the best mindset. My dad was still Barney—but he was also Barney that was hungover, and I knew what that looks like. He was quiet and kind of puttering around and doing his thing. I knew he was hurting, and the last thing I wanted to do was trigger something within him and piss him off. I know that during my drinking days, when I was hungover, I didn't want any kind of conflict, and I sensed that from him now. So I just stayed happy and went through the motions.

Later, when we were packing up to leave, I said to Jen that this wasn't going to be the last time we came to Brandon. Our kids were going to grow up knowing about Uncle Terence and where he took his last footsteps. Now we could come back with joy and without having a cloud over us, because we had been able to confront those emotions head-on and move forward. Every time we have an opportunity to go back, we're going to go back and reminisce and talk about our time there.

Leaving Brandon that day was bittersweet. I remember jumping on the highway and telling myself, "This could be the last time driving on this highway for a lot of years. I'm just going to sit here and soak it in in silence and internalize everything that I've gone through emotionally and physically."

But I knew that someday we would be back. The next time we go there, I want to make a point of going back to where it all went down for Terence. I'll be able to do that with pride and with joy, celebrating my brother's life and not going there scared.

We spent a few days in Winnipeg before heading home to Kelowna. I talked to my mother there. "I can't believe I was able to be present and sane, and not lose my mind through that," she said. I could really sense the relief that she felt.

And my dad? That's a tough one. With him, everything is surface stuff. I know he likes to internalize everything. In Brandon, all he could say to me was that I should stand tall and be proud. "You accomplished a lot," he said. But nothing was said about what happened with Terence because he just doesn't want to go there.

When my dad has a little bit of clarity, he's a positive person, at least on the outside. But I know he was hurting and boiling inside. It's hard . . . the emotions. I hope the experience was good for him. "Make sure you call Mom every other day," he said to me when I said goodbye. "You know, she's going through a tough time."

And I thought, "If only you would realize what you're putting her through. Maybe it's time you slowed down."

But you can't teach an old dog new tricks. You can only do what you can do. It's up to them to figure it out. I was grateful that everyone was able to make it to Brandon, and now it was up to them to take what they wanted from the experience and use it as a positive light.

12 We All Fight a Fight No One Knows About

Mind over matter. Those were my brother Terence's words. When I was young, it never really occurred to me what he was talking about, but over the years I've come to understand what he meant.

Terence was always the one leading the charge. He wasn't physically the biggest guy, but that idea of mind over matter had been instilled in him since he was a young boy. He *had* to think that way. He surpassed boundaries that you'd never think he could surpass. Driving a snowmobile in minus-fifty. Having to haul caribou meat for miles in summer while battling the mosquitoes.

When he was still in grade school, my parents sent Terence out to work to make money for the family. He shovelled snow in the winter and then he became a janitor for a company owned by some family friends that cleaned all the government buildings in Rankin Inlet. It would be fucking midnight on a school night and he'd still be working.

A lot of nights, he would also have to deal with Dad and bring him home. Terence was only twelve or thirteen years old and it was minus-forty outside. He would get home at three in the morning with Dad on the back of the Ski-Doo, and the yelling and screaming would start and there would be a huge ruckus. Then, after Dad was fed, we'd put him to sleep. He'd wake up the next day and it would be like fuck all happened.

But Terence would still have to go back and finish cleaning the buildings, even if it was three in the morning. I don't know how he did it.

"It's mind over matter, right?" he'd say.

Whether it was hunting or playing hockey or dealing with Dad, you could always count on him because he got it done. He would put himself in vulnerable situations, but he took that chance because he believed he was strong enough to get through whatever pain was in front of him.

When Terence left after Grade 10 to play AAA midget hockey in Thompson, Manitoba, I had to take on the snow shovelling job, and also the role of babysitting my dad. I isolated myself in my room a lot and kind of stayed out of sight until Mom would come wake me up and tell me, "You need to go pick him up."

Looking back now, I realize I was taken advantage of by my parents, at least in my eyes.

In the winter, Mom would wake me up at 6 a.m. "You've got to go to work," she'd say. I had to get my two hours of snow shovelling in. I'd get up with no breakfast—nothing. Put my parka on. Go outside. Ski-Doo won't start because it's so cold? Well, fuck . . . I'd go back inside, get a bucket of hot water, bring it out and splash it on the carburetor and start the machine. I learned that trick by watching Terence.

I'd have seven buildings to shovel out—seven government buildings. It was pitch-black outside. I would be out there in that darkness, afraid of being alone, the winds howling. I'd get through the first building and on to the second. By that time, I was freezing my ass off, but I had to get it done because I couldn't be late for school. Eight o'clock would come around, and cars were starting to move around town. I finally got home around 8:20, and then left for school by 8:30. There was minimal food in my stomach. I was already burnt out physically and mentally. I'd have a full day of school and then go home to deal with whatever shit was happening before Dad got home from his work as a plumber.

Monday, Wednesday and Friday, I had hockey practice after dinner. And then the cycle was repeated.

I didn't tell any of my friends that I was working shovelling snow. I guess I was embarrassed. I remember wishing the snow would never, ever come again. I'd look outside the night before— "Fuck, it's snowing, got to get up." "Fuck, Dad's out partying. I might have to go out and bring him home." But whatever happened, I had to do the work and then get the paycheque, and then not even see the fucking paycheque—my mom controlled the bank account and how we spent the money. My parents became dependent on what Terence and I made.

I did that by myself for two years. The job became almost an escape and a release from the reality in our home. It got to the point where I was doing it fucking mad. I wanted to get the biggest chunk of snow I could handle and throw it as far as I could. There was a lot of anger, and over time that built up inside me. But at least I had hockey, where I could go out and smack someone around. Otherwise, I felt trapped. It was like I couldn't, didn't, have any feelings for anything.

Over time, it just became normal. People ask me how I did it. Well, fuck, you've got to do what you've got to do.

We all fight a fight no one knows about, and we don't always win. Unless you've experienced failure, devastating failure, you don't know what it is to get knocked down and then pick yourself back up again.

You set yourself up to become successful by accepting failure. That's what creates mental toughness.

In today's age, people don't want to accept failure. This younger generation want to know the outcome before they put one foot in the door.

I jumped in. I knew ever since I was a young kid that in order to grow, you have to experience that gut-wrenching feeling of being knocked down. I hate the feeling of defeat. It sucks the life out of you. But in order to keep going, you have to be able to realize that no one in this world lives a perfect life. You learn by your mistakes. It's all about life experience. It's not about the information that you read off paper; it's the feeling. How are you ever supposed to learn if you don't put yourself out there?

I've been around many people who just can't accept failure, and when they do fail at something, they feel like it's the end of the world.

When you become comfortable and content in your own skin and realize we don't have to be perfect human beings, when you get through the experience and the outcome is not what you expected it to be, you take those little baby steps and battle through.

Like Terence said, mind over matter . . .

My brother was the most nurturing figure in my life, especially when I was a kid. He kind of played both the male and female parenting role for me that I didn't get from my mother and father. But there were also others.

Simone Clark was my teacher when I was in Grade 8, and she was one of the most important people for me from the time I started school until the time I left to play hockey and go to high school in Alberta. It wasn't until adulthood that I looked back and reflected and realized how much she helped me get through those difficult days.

Simone and her husband, Donald, who is also a teacher, moved to Rankin Inlet from New Brunswick. A lot of the people who come to teach in the Far North are from the south. When Donald and Simone came to Nunavut, they were young and inexperienced and they knew that other life—the southern life. But they became part of the community right from the get-go. Southerners have to take on the Northern lifestyle in order to survive. A lot of them, whether they're teachers or government workers, can't do it, and just turn around and leave after a year or two. Simone and Donald embraced it, and that earned them a lot of respect within our community. They're still there today.

Looking back, I realize that a lot of the teachers who came from the south really put their work in to help the kids who were struggling. The local teachers knew what was going on behind closed doors, but they just did their job and kept their lips shut because they were probably dealing with the same shit in their own homes. When you're from a small community, people hold grudges. So, the local teachers hold back from saying anything or exposing anyone because they're afraid that people are going to say things about them and rumours are going to spread. It's unfortunate.

Simone and Donald had three kids who were the same ages as me and my brother and sister, and we all grew up together. I felt like part of their extended family. Their daughter Kelly was in the same grade as me, starting in kindergarten, and took me under her wing. I wasn't the quickest learner. Kelly always kept me up to par when I felt like I was struggling. It was almost like she knew when I was dealing with trouble at home. I don't know if she had a conversations with her mom.

Simone had an intuition about me from the time I was a young kid. I don't want to say I was favoured by her, because she had that extra time to give to a lot of her students. She and Donald understood that there was a lot of dysfunction in a lot of our homes. When you're a teacher, you can spot those students who are struggling.

But with me, right away, she just had that motherly instinct. I remember her always having time and doing those little things that might go unnoticed for a lot of people.

She was my safe person. I wasn't the smartest kid in class. And I was a kid who didn't have a voice. I had no concept of how to communicate. I always felt like I was never good enough, and that showed in my school work. I struggled a lot with instructions, but Simone helped build me up to be resilient and push through. She knew about the hockey talent I had, and she helped me overcome a lot of my fears. If it wasn't for her pulling me aside constantly and asking how I was doing, there's no chance I would have got through.

I'd show up at school, looking dead tired, and in Simone's eyes I could tell she was thinking, "Jordin had to look after Barney last night." Terence had already left to play hockey by then so my dad was my responsibility.

Playing hockey was a different story. I was the best in town. I had no issues with confidence on the ice. It freed me. It was almost like I put a shield around myself and there was nothing else except me on the ice. There's no way I would ever admit being the best at that age. But now, looking back, I'm able to say yeah, I was the best, at least in our town. I was a very shy, timid guy who didn't want to be in the spotlight, but in hockey my name started to become known.

I was always looking to shift the spotlight to my teammates. I had hundreds of opportunities to score goals, but I just gave them to my teammates so that they could get the glory.

I remember the time when we went to a tournament in Yellowknife when we were peewees—eleven, twelve years old. We were going into the final game. I looked over at our goalie, Dustin, and he had his head down.

"I don't know if I can do this," he said.

"No. Dustin, you're the best fucking goalie here," I told him. "Let's go win. You're the best."

A light bulb went on for him, and we went out and won the tournament. I knew a bit of Dustin's family story—a white dad and an Inuk mom, substance abuse, a lot of dysfunction. I knew we were kind of on the same page. But from that tournament on, he was our guy. I think it really helped him break through his shell of not believing in himself. I told him, "I believe in you. I know you're the best here." And he was our top goalie in minor hockey until I left.

But in the classroom, I was tight-lipped. I didn't trust myself, didn't trust my ability to do the work. It's almost like I was a couple of years behind everyone else, learning-wise. But Simone always instilled confidence in me.

At first, I thought it was weird. "Why is she focusing on me?" Not so much visibly in front of the whole class, but at the end of class she would ask me, "Jordin, do you need help with anything?" I'd fail tests, and she would pull me aside and help me redo them.

My mind was still at home with fucking everything that was going on, and I just couldn't focus on school. She would tell me to take a deep breath—"You're here, you're safe, concentrate on this." And I got through it.

Our relationship extended beyond school. I'd show up at their place all the time. I would literally sit in her living room, silent for hours on end, and she would just be in her rocking chair and look back at me. She knew I was scared, but she helped push me to go overcome that fear because she knew the situation that I was in. I felt like she believed I had potential.

I'd be sitting at her house on a Friday night and her phone would ring. Simone would answer, and on the other end it would be my mom yelling, "Tell Jordin he needs to get his fucking ass home." There was tension between my mom and Simone, maybe because my mom felt a little disregarded as a mother.

I can remember Simone taking a deep breath and sighing and saying, "Jordin, the phone is for you. It's your mom." Oh shit, here we go again. Embarrassment set in, and then I would just kind of slowly ninja out the door and walk home with my tail between my legs. "What am I going to get in shit for now?" As I was leaving, Simone would always say, "Jordin, make sure you look after yourself." It was nothing directly related to what was going on at home, but you could tell—she knew.

I grew up with a lot of yelling. Now I catch myself when I start to raise my voice towards my kids and think, "Fuck, why did I just do that? Why can't I have a normal conversation?" The kind of conversations the Clarks had with their kids or my buddy Troy's mom, Margo, had with Troy and his sister? That was unfamiliar territory to me.

Every time I was over at Simone's house, there was a sense of calm, of peace in the way she talked to me. And I always felt

This journey all began here: out on the land, where things seem clearer. I was with my friend and agent, Mike Watson. We've been through a lot together.

The news of unmarked graves at residential schools put a spotlight on a history of trauma in this country. Those reports brought a lot of grief to the surface and also helped many people make sense of the past. I think the people whose families—like mine—had been affected by the residential school experience bore the brunt of that trauma, but have a new chance now to understand how that past has impacted their lives.

Jennifer came back into my life when I was ready to get my act together. I am grateful every day that she did.

Our wedding probably wasn't typical. We had three strong contingents. Sicilians, Inuit, and a bunch of NHLers. There could have been fireworks, but it all came off without incident.

In good times and bad, the most important thing is family. I owe everything to my parents, and I make sure every day to be the kind of dad my kids can look up to. Thanks, Mom and Dad, for teaching me so much.

I think just about any parent would say the same thing: having kids will make you a better person. Siena and Avery have changed my world, and brought Jennifer and me a kind of joy we didn't know existed.

In many ways, this book is about my dad. He went through so much, the kind of thing that echoes from generation to generation. But he has taught me a lot. I wouldn't be the man I am without him.

That is Terence, the guy who first told me that "mind over matter" is the way to get through tough times. He inspires me to this day.

weird about those situations because I had never had that with my own mother. In our home there was just a lot of yelling and screaming and a lot of anger.

When Simone and her family sat down for dinner, there was a conversation.

When I left Rankin at age fourteen to go and play hockey in Spruce Grove, Alberta, Simone flew her whole family down to watch one of my games. My own parents never did that. It was at that point that I realized they were like family to me. I was having a tough time being away from home; she was giving me that extra push to stay, showing her belief in me.

Now, when I go back to Rankin Inlet and see her, she always has the biggest smile on her face. I can feel her pride in me.

I mentioned my buddy Troy's mom, Margo. She was the other strong female influence in my life. Troy and I were born two days apart and have been friends since day one. Ever since I can remember, Margo has always been there.

Troy lost his father to suicide when he was a little kid. I don't know very much about what happened; it was never talked about. But I do know that Troy grew up with a lot of questions. He never really had a father figure in his life, so my father became his, although from a very limited perspective because, growing up, he only saw the good side of my dad. Troy always looked up to my father in a positive way until, in adulthood, he realized what kind of human being my dad can become.

At the same time, Troy's home was always a safe home for me, and Troy's mom was an important influence in my life. Margo was a schoolteacher for thirty-plus years. She never used alcohol or drugs. I relished my time at their place. It was a calm environment that was so different from my own home. I always envied Troy having a mother like that.

Without a doubt, Margo knew what was going on in my household. She took a little extra care with my brother and me every time we came over. Nearly every weekend, I found an excuse to sleep over at Troy's house. Even on some weekdays I would sleep there. (Thinking back, just about all of my sleepovers were at my friends' houses. They weren't ever at my place, for obvious reasons.)

I can remember one time when I was about eleven or twelve years old and things started firing up at our house on a Friday evening. Troy was out of town for some reason, but even though I knew he wasn't there, I pretended I didn't, and called Margo asking if it would be okay for me to sleep over and be with Troy. It was an excuse, and she knew it. She understood exactly why I was calling on a Friday night. My parents were in an uproar and I needed an escape.

It's hard to describe the chaos of those nights at home with all of the random outbursts. I was constantly getting in shit all the time for no reason. As soon as the bottle was pulled out, you knew it was eventually going to happen—the yelling and screaming and physical and verbal abuse. Arguments would start between my parents, and eventually the kids got in the middle of it. That was just the norm. You start to recognize the steps before the blow-up happens. And you know when it's time to get out—before things start to really get heated up.

"Come on over," Margo said. "I've got a movie and popcorn." I remember clearly as a twelve-year-old, sitting there in silence and so zoned in on the movie—it was *The Mighty Ducks*, right after it first came out.

The next day I went home and knew that as soon as I walked in the door, I'd get shit as though it was all my fault. There was this Catch-22—whether I stayed or I went, I was going to get in shit either way. When you're three sheets to the wind, I don't think you remember anything. But my parents would wake up in the morning, notice I wasn't there and assume I'd gone somewhere for the night.

"How dare you do that? This is our home—you stay home." They had no real idea what had happened the night before because they were blacked out, but as a young kid I was too fearful to tell the truth. When you grow up in fear, you learn early on that less is more.

Margo was so supportive. She just had that calm presence about her, and she still does to this day. I will always remember how she cared about the youth in our community. She knew what was going on in a lot of homes.

She's retired and living in Winnipeg now. She's still a joy to be around.

Over the years, I have developed my own rules to live by. They are based on my experiences, based on what I learned from my brother and from those other people who influenced me. They may seem harsh to you, and they may not work the same for everyone. But for me, they make sense.

The Jordin Rules

SIX THINGS NATURALLY STRONG PEOPLE DO

1. They move on. They don't waste time.
2. They embrace change. They welcome challenges.
3. They stay happy. They don't waste energy on things they can't control.
4. They are kind, fair, and unafraid to speak up.
5. They are willing to take calculated risks.
6. They celebrate other people's success. They don't resent that success.

MY TWELVE RULES FOR SUCCESS

1. Do the fucking work. Don't be lazy.
2. Stop fucking waiting. It's time.
3. Rely on yourself. The universe doesn't give a fuck.
4. Be fucking practical. Success is not a theory.
5. Be productive early. Don't fuck around all day.
6. Don't be a fucking baby. Life's hard. Get on with it.
7. Don't hang out with fuckwits.
8. Don't waste energy on shit you can't control.
9. Stop bullshitting. It's fucking embarrassing.

10. Stop being a fucking people-pleaser. It's sad.
11. Stop doing the same fucking thing and hoping shit will change.

THREE WAYS TO FAIL AT EVERYTHING IN LIFE

1. Blame your problems on others.
2. Complain about everything.
3. Be ungrateful.

13 I Am Who I Am Because We Are

A couple of years ago, I was on the road, in a hotel, on one of my trips for a speaking engagement. When I'm alone at night on my own, it's my chance to catch up on watching television. I flipped on Netflix and happened to stumble on a series called *The Playbook: A Coach's Rules for Life*. It was about famous coaches in different sports. I played the first episode about Doc Rivers, who is a basketball coach in the NBA.

I knew the name, but I didn't know much about him. What I saw that night gave me a new way to think not just about sports but also about life.

Rivers was talking about when he coached the Boston Celtics to the NBA championship in 2008. That was a team with three superstars: Kevin Garnett, Paul Pierce and Ray Allen. Rivers told a story about how a lady came up to him and told him the Celtics were going to be a great team, and then asked if he had ever heard of ubuntu.

Then the show cut to a clip of Archbishop Desmond Tutu speaking in South Africa.

"We have something in our African community, something that is very difficult to put into English. It is called ubuntu," he said. "Ubuntu is the essence of being human. It says a solitary human is a contradiction in terms. I have to learn from other human beings how to be human."

Then Rivers explained what that meant to him.

"A person is a person through other people. I can't be all I can be unless you are all you can be. I can never be threatened by you because you are good, because the better you are, the better I am."

He said that he brought the concept of ubuntu to his players, and when they bought into it, that's what turned them from a group of talented individuals into a championship team.

I couldn't get to sleep that night. I was thinking, "How can I instil this in our Indigenous communities?" I don't want to be put on a pedestal. I want my success to be shared by our people. I want to uplift them because they have uplifted me. The starting point for all of us is the same: I am who I am because we are.

We have many superstars. But we have to be able to let go of our ego, let our pride down a little bit and acknowledge that we all need to care for each other. In order for us to have success, not one or two or three people are going to do it for us—we are all going to have to do it together.

———

I started doing public speaking when I was eighteen or nineteen years old and still playing junior hockey in Brandon. After I got to the NHL, every off-season I would do a week-long tour of the Far North. I'd go to six or seven communities and share my experiences.

I admit there was a real disconnect. I'd go into these events hungover, probably smelling like booze, and talk about how bad drugs and alcohol were. The first five or six years of my public-speaking venture, I was basically lying to my audience and lying to myself.

I would look out into the crowd and see a lot of desperate eyes looking for help from one of their own. At the time, I didn't realize how much pressure was being put on me because I was in a fog myself. I was being looked to to fix everything for everyone else, and for that day that I was there, I felt like a hero. One individual is not going to fucking take the whole haul for everyone, but I felt the responsibility was on me to show our people the better way of living, just by my actions.

Then, after an event, I always had two or three people who had a couple of bottles waiting for me to help me get to bed at night. I needed that bottle of booze to unwind.

When I left the community the next day, I kind of wiped my hands and said, "I've done my job." On to the next one.

After I sobered up I started looking back and realized how I hadn't been true to myself. It took five or six years into sobriety to really be comfortable and content in my own skin and live out the words that I was sharing with our people on how to live a healthy life.

There's no fucking manual or script on how to live your life, and nobody lives a perfect life—if you think you do, it's fake shit. We all have issues.

One of my main points is that we all need to look ourselves in the mirror and ask ourselves, "Am I the best version of myself?" That's where ubuntu comes in. I want to be able to walk into any First Nations community and say, "I am who I am because we are."

After every event, I get a lot of positive feedback. People tell me they see light at the end of the tunnel and that I am giving them hope. I'm not a doctor and I'm not a psychologist. What I have is lived experience. For a lot of our people, when they're told to see a therapist, there's no connection there for them. There's no lived experience. These therapists are taking what they know out of a textbook, and that's not how our people live. That's why for many years it was hard for me to connect with a therapist. They had no understanding of the way we grew up.

When I share my story with our people—I don't want to sound cocky or anything, but they look to me for answers. Not someone telling them you've got to do this, this is how you should live—that's what we've been told for our whole lives. All of those voices telling them that, in order to be successful, you have to live like this, you have to do this.

To us, success is survival, and we want to hear things in black and white.

When I'm up onstage, I can look into the audience and pick out the people who are battling inner demons. When I start talking about my experiences with my parents and I look at parents in the crowd, a lot of heads are down and a lot of people walk out because it's hitting them right in their fucking heart. But that's what our people need to hear more of. Our children don't know how to relay their experiences and their thoughts because that conversation doesn't happen in their homes—just like it didn't happen when I was growing up. But the parents fucking know. A lot of times in these remote communities, you see children running wild in the streets and the parents say they don't have control of their kids. Well, fuck, what happens in your home? It's not your child's fault that they're out of control. It's because there is a lot of dysfunction in the home.

It's not just about putting shame or guilt on parents. It's allowing them to absorb what their kids are experiencing through my talking about my experience with my parents.

I usually do a meet and greet after my speech, and man, I've had a few tears in my eyes because of the stories that were shared by some of the kids. I was reliving my own childhood listening to them. They tell me, "My parents are lost causes. They beat me. They verbally abuse me." Those same parents would come through the line later on, and I wouldn't cause a scene or anything, but I would ask them, "Are you being true to yourself? Are you giving your kids the best opportunity?" Right away, I could see it in their eyes. You read people through their eyes and their facial expressions—little things.

I make a point on every trip to tell parents they need to give their kids an opportunity to change. Set your ego and your pride aside. It's not the child's fault that you are the way you are. Playing the victim will only take you so far.

I have had some memorable experiences on those trips. I remember one time I was invited to speak on the Six Nations reserve near Brantford, Ontario—Stan Jonathan's neck of the woods. They had a community liaison who was driving me around with the chief to meet different people. It's pretty common. Usually the chief takes you around, and you start by going to his cousin's house or something like that.

They told me about this one teenager in the community who had locked himself in his home for two years. I think about him all the time now. The chief asked me if we could go and have a chat with the boy. I was kind of nervous myself, but I didn't show it. I said, "Yeah, absolutely, let's go over to his house. Maybe I can be the one to help him." But I didn't really know what I was getting into.

I remember walking into the house, and it was dead fucking silent. There were a bunch of family members sitting on the couch. No words needed to be said. I knocked on the teenager's bedroom door. The kid was massively overweight. And I just sat there and chatted with him about my experience and what I have been through. I was there for about an hour.

When I got home a couple of days later, that chief called me and told me that the young man had finally come out of his room and was able to gain the confidence he needed to make that first step.

That one really made me look in the mirror and say, "Wow. If on all of these trips that I'm doing I can help one person get out of that black hole, I've done my job."

On another trip, I went to Alert Bay, just off Vancouver Island. I had become really good friends with the chief there, who is an ex-athlete, a soccer player. We connected really well. He's been sober now for five years. I remember he said to me, "Your experience is mine."

The chief told me there were a few young people in his community who could really use some words of wisdom. I crave those moments of being able to help these young kids get out of a rut.

There was this one teenage girl who was so shy because she experienced things that were hard for her to share. I was able to connect with her. It was the first time she had ever got out in public and put her face out there. We chatted about surface stuff. There were tons of people around, so it was kind of hard for her to delve into personal experiences. I don't need the details. The details don't matter as long as I'm there physically for them. But I knew what she was feeling, and ultimately that's what it's all about. What they have experienced is probably much worse than what I have experienced.

After I talked, I gave her a hug. She was shaking.

The chief called me a couple of weeks later. The girl had written a letter saying how she could see life from a different perspective because of that visit. Hearing that really filled my heart.

——

After every public event, I get a lot of feedback through email or social media—people telling me about coming to the realization that there is a better life. I want to be able to help people, to educate people. I love going to communities not because they're putting me on this pedestal—I don't look at it as that. I go to those places because I am one of them. That's how you become accepted by our people—when you treat everyone equally. That's why people are comfortable around me. I happen to have been able to live out my dreams and overcome my hardships. But I'm still the same as you. I'm your cousin. Knowing that helps a lot of them let their guard down.

Sometimes Aboriginal people can be their own worst enemy, especially when jealousy kicks in. When someone is successful among our people, others often want to take them down. It's like the whole community turns against that person or that family. All these groups and cliques join forces and there are a lot of grudges. We have to get to the point where we realize that each and every one of us has a special gift, and when that special gift comes to light, you want other people to share in your success. The community has to get on board and let go of that ego and that narcissism. And if you don't like it, put your head down and put in the fucking work and accomplish something yourself. I found my path, which happened to be hockey. But there are others.

I see the trap that they're in because of the generational stuff. Grandparents telling grandchildren, "Don't ever leave home. You're the next leader . . ." They're taught, "What's the point of leaving? You're surviving here."

Substance abuse, domestic abuse, all that shit is not normal. But it's normalized in a lot of these remote villages and communities. It frustrates me when I see kids who are excited to leave to become tradesmen, to go to college or university. The first month in, it's all fine and dandy, and then they hit a wall and their family tells them, "Well, just come home. Everything's better at home."

In order to expand your thoughts, you have to go outside the box and look from the outside in.

And sometimes it's our own leaders who let us down.

It sparks a fire in me when I visit First Nations communities and I'm around leaders and see how selfish they are. I've been a fly on the wall listening to band members and councillors, and I shake my head a lot. I'm steaming inside because I want to call them out. I see decisions that are made based on how they will boost their families or friends rather than being for the benefit of the whole community. Certain council members' families might own a business, and they get first crack at opportunities. A lot of them have prominent last names, and they are the ones making the decisions based on their own interests rather than looking at the poorer families and thinking about how they can lift them up.

At the same time, those leaders are telling me that life is great on their reserve. There were a couple of trips where the band wanted to rent a helicopter and give me a tour. These are leaders who want to show off to their community and say, "Look what I did—what *I* did—for Jordin Tootoo," rather than saying, "We as people need to give our kids better opportunities, so let's spend our money wisely."

Guys, take that fifteen or twenty grand, whatever it's going to cost to rent a helicopter for an hour-long tour, and put it towards the kids. I don't need to see an aerial view.

When you speak about responsibility, the problem is that many of our parents and political leaders have never experienced being responsible themselves. So, how are they going to teach their own kids or look after their people? That's one of the after-effects of generational trauma. The older generation believes it's not their responsibility to be a better person because so many governments fucked them over. I understand why that is. In the past, we were told that the government or the church was going to help us, and instead they fucked us. Now, for people on a lot of the reserves, it's hard for them to get over that hump and accept outsiders coming in to help them—by outsiders I mean the white political establishment.

A lot of our people are also afraid of living a different life. We need to shift the mindset. We have to stop constantly playing the victim, and thinking it's always everyone else's fault. We've been saying this for decades as Indigenous people, and it's going to take time to change. It's not going to happen overnight. And I understand how we've already been waiting for years for things to change. But we as Indigenous people have to take that step forward. We have to take the onus upon ourselves to change. No one else is going to do it for us. We've got to be able to listen and hear the stories from our elders, the people who experienced those hardships, who were in the residential schools. We think life is hard in this generation? Fuck, people have no idea what our parents and grandparents went through. And the fact is that our people don't know how to share their experiences because they've always been told to shut up, put your head down and walk away.

But we also have trouble helping—and accepting help from—our own people. We've got to come together as one nation and not have all these grudges and feuds within our communities and towns. The reserves need to work together. I see things in the Okanagan, near where I live in Kelowna— one band has a lot of resources, and the band next to them lives in a rundown place. Why not help each other out?

What I hear over and over again is people saying, "We can do it on our own. We will do it our way." That's why you have those walls between reserves who are next to each other. Their filters are high. We are taught to do it our own way. You guys have your success and think you're better than us? We'll do it our own way. A lot of successful reserves are reaching out and trying to help, but that help is not accepted, and that's a problem. It's like getting sober. When you accept the help that's offered, life begins again. As long as you don't accept it, nothing is going to change.

A lot of our people don't want to hear the fucking truth. My words may sound harsh, but that's the reality.

During my visits to First Nations communities, it feels like everyone is happy while I'm there, everyone is looking forward to it, but it's the work that gets done after I leave that really matters. Changing a cycle requires a sacrifice. That's where it's the hardest. It's like sobriety. You've experienced that life of using, but in sobriety you've got to live a completely new life, and when it gets too hard, you tend to revert to what was easy for you. That's when relapse happens.

In a lot of these communities, everyone's on a high note when I'm there, but when I leave and things start to get tough and seem too overwhelming, they revert. That way of life has been normalized. You learn as young kids to live with what's in front of you, when in reality there's so much more out there for you. These young kids, the youth, they don't know any better. But the problem is when the parents are suffering themselves—what's going to happen? The cycle is just going to continue. It's sad to see.

When I leave after my visits, when I fly or drive away, I sit in silence and think, "Fuck, man, all these kids have no hope." But maybe one or two people changed their mindset.

I'm not coming in to tell them how to fix their community. That's impossible for one person to do. They need to uplift each other rather than playing the victim or bringing other people down. That's where ubuntu comes in. That's where we really have to start believing, I am who I am because we are.

It has to come from within. This is a letter I received after my first book was published. When I read something like this, it gives me hope.

Dear Jordin Tootoo,
My name is Kylie Lariviere and I'm seventeen years old. I am a hockey player who has a dream of playing university hockey.

I am reaching out to you to tell you that I have recently read your book for my English class and for my final project in Social Studies. Before reading the book I figured that I would do something about Indigenous peoples' mental health in sports or the things they face to get a brave and strong mindset. Your book really hit close to home and had an impact on me. I can't say I have dealt with a lot of the things that you have dealt with but there are a few familiar situations. I want to share my story with you that I haven't been able to share with anyone else.

I come from the English River First Nation: Patuanak is a small isolated reserve in Northern Saskatchewan. Up North, there isn't that much to do, just go out to the parts of our land where we do cultural activity with the elders and the adults who have experience. We go fishing on the lake, cut or get some wood, go rip around with buddies on our quads or Ski-Doos, you know the same old things people do on the reserve. The thing that kills our community the most is alcohol and drugs. Everyone is dealing or has dealt with alcohol and drug abuse in their life, and everyone has tried it, mostly starting from when they were twelve or thirteen, and I'm not going to lie here, I tried both. When I first tried alcohol I was fourteen. I was living in Banff at the time to play hockey. I was the youngest on the team so I got peer pressured into it and I honestly didn't enjoy it. I was fifteen when I tried weed. I was with my brother during that time. When COVID first hit, we were sent home, but I didn't want to go home, so my time being there was worse than it already had been. I was told that it would take away my stress, anxiety, etc. But it for sure had an impact on me for the next few months. My reserve, when I was growing up, was so beautiful to me. I would be so happy to go back knowing I would see my grandparents, my cousins, and everyone else. I was mostly excited to see my grandmother though.

My grandmother will forever be my biggest inspiration. When I was younger she would always take care of me while my parents were being parents, a shoulder to cry on, a person to rant or talk to about things, but she was my go-to person for anything. That all changed when we found out she had gotten diagnosed with cancer in 2017. It was the most painful news to hear. The one thing I hated myself for is that I barely spent time with her during that time. But before I could tell her all the good things that were starting to go well in my life, she passed away in July 2018. My heart was broken, the people in our community broke, she was known and loved in all the northern communities, she was such a kind-hearted person to anyone she met, she was humble about herself and she cared so much for her grandchildren, and with me being the oldest grandchild, it hurt me the most. That's when everything started to go downhill for my family and me.

Growing up, I lived in a caring and loving home,

but once I realized what alcohol did to my parents, the environment in my home changed. I was only three. There would be yelling happening all night and it would go till two in the afternoon the next day. Before my brother was born, it was just me. It was rough having to live with the yelling almost every free weekend they had together. Having to call the police just to get them to stop fighting was tough. At school, some days I would have to make my own lunch, walk to school by myself or try to keep my cool during school. I went to an English/French immersion school with a bunch of white kids, and I was bullied some days, but the ones who bullied me didn't like me because they knew I played sports and that I was better than them, not to sound cocky or anything.

The thing I hated the most was that my parents were never able to control their alcohol, so most nights while my mom would be passed out, my dad would be up doing things that traumatized me. I don't want to get into much further detail with it. When my brother, Deacon came into the picture in 2011, it was just him and me. We would be home by ourselves while the yelling was happening. As the oldest child, it was tough, mostly having to take care of my brother and myself while I was trying to break up fights at only eight years old and my brother was one. See, when things would go out of control, that's when I would call my grandparents. It was mostly my grandma, Gloria, who would drive the six hours to come and take Deacon and me. It felt like the only time I had actually had sober parents before Deacon was born was when I had school events happening, when the family would come over, road trips, when my dad was at work and my mom would be at university, or especially during any time that I had hockey.

Growing up, the arena would be my home, knowing that there wasn't going to be any fighting, no yelling at me, no touching me, it was my escape from reality, my go-to anger release. I have been playing hockey for thirteen years and I have also been playing in the CSSHL league for four years. I am currently living in Penticton, British Columbia, and playing for the Okanagan Hockey Academy for my final year of minor hockey. The past couple of years, for the 18/19–19/20 seasons, I got the chance to live in my "dream place to live," Banff, to play for the Banff Hockey Academy. In Edmonton for the 20/21 season, I got to play for the Northern Alberta Extreme. Hockey has always been there for me, but it's been hard these past couple of years. Having so much pressure on me on and off the ice from everyone, especially my dad, has been a tough go for me. I get it that they want me to succeed and to do my best, but it's been mentally and physically challenging and draining. Every day I try my best and I just push through. I was always hesitant to ask or to try to find help because I tend to ball up the things in my life and let all of it get the best of me, but once I reached out to the academic advisor of the Okanagan Hockey Academy at the school I started becoming more comfortable with him and my teachers. I finally had the courage to speak out and try to find some help. I would never have written this letter to you if it weren't for David Nackoney, or for reading your book.

My little life story has come to an end. I would love to talk about more of the things I did and had dealt with growing up, but if I were to, it would be too much of a read and would be the length as its own non-fiction book as well. I am beyond grateful that you have taken the time to read my story. It doesn't seem like much at all but it's truly a lot to me. I never got to talk about some of the things I've talked about here. I really hope I get the chance to write a book like you someday. Once I graduate from university, my plan is to talk about my story because you are such an inspiration to me and to many Indigenous peoples around North America, and if I ever have the chance to write my own book, I want all the youth, especially the Indigenous girls in sports, to never be afraid to speak out whenever they need to, because I started to speak out these past couple of months and it's gotten better and easier for me. It's taken me seventeen years to talk about my past, but I'm so glad I did.

Yours truly, Kylie Lariviere

14 I Used It as Motivation

The topic of racism in hockey is finally being talked about openly, mostly because of Akim Aliu and the incidents he reported with his former coach Bill Peters, and more recently, what happened to P.K. Subban's brother Jordan while he was playing in the ECHL.

When all of that stuff started to come out, I guarantee you there were a lot of coaches and former coaches out there who were walking with their tails between their legs because they were afraid something was going to come out. Those are the guys that can't get to sleep at night right now.

It was great to see all the information come into the public eye, but it wasn't news to me. Racism has always been part of the sport, whether you're Indigenous, brown or Black.

I first experienced it when I left home in Rankin Inlet to play hockey in Spruce Grove when I was fourteen years old.

Before that, I can honestly say that growing up in Nunavut, I had never experienced racism, to the point where my team-mates and coaches in Alberta had to kind of educate me about what people were saying to me. It kind of went in one ear and out the other. I had no idea.

What I first noticed were the parents in the stands who didn't know right from wrong. They would be shouting out stuff about how I must have lied about my age, about how "Indians" were always looking for a free ride. Indigenous people were looked at as using the race card to make other people feel sorry for them or to gain an advantage. But I didn't know the history back then. What were they talking about?

When it started to sink in, that was the first time I looked at myself in the mirror and asked myself, "Is this sport really for me? Why am I being targeted racially?"

There was a lot more of that in junior hockey and when I got to the pros. Emotions run high and guys will do whatever it takes to take an opponent down mentally, take them off their game. I got a lot of "You're a savage" or "Go back to where you belong. You don't belong down here. You're an animal."

When you hear guys chirping like that from the bench, you might wonder if some coaches were involved. Those guys know who they are.

I got a lot of verbal abuse, but I used it as motivation. I stood my ground. I was always taught to never back down and to stand up for myself. And violence was the way I had to do it.

Nobody wanted to talk about it. Everything was swept under the rug by the officials or the management team. There were a lot of times where someone said, "We'll handle it internally" or this or that, but you knew nothing was going to happen.

I'm not trying to expose anyone. Those people know who they are. It's a waste of my energy to start pointing fingers and naming names and playing the blame game because I've lived it my whole life and I'm over that shit. I've moved on. But there were a couple of incidents in the minors that I will never forget.

I dreaded being sent down because I knew I was going to face way more racism there. Compared to the NHL, the AHL and ECHL are a whole different ballgame. A lot of shit goes down there. There are a lot more corrupt individuals running the show, and those corrupt individuals are selfish fucks. The players are just a herd of cows being shuffled around.

When you're on the visiting team, you go into every rink wondering, "When is it going to happen?" Beginning of the game, end of the game? I knew that it was going to happen eventually because of the way that I played. My style made guys mad, so I knew what was coming back my way, and that was in the back of my head every night. I felt it more in sobriety, when I started analyzing each fucking sentence that was said to me by guys trying to get me off my game.

I had always played the same style. I looked at it as being the Tasmanian devil on ice, the guy who stirred shit up but was able to fucking back himself up. I don't think I would have ever been the player that I was if I didn't have that little crazy side of my brain, being able to drop the mitts and put my life on the line for my teammates.

The only times I would ever get jittery were when the media would overblow something that happened three games ago, and now we were playing the same team again. You'd get off the ice after the pre-game skate and the media would be all over you—"Do you remember what happened? Do you think something is going to happen tonight?" Well, fuck, of course it's going to happen at some point, whether I took a cheap shot at someone or someone took a cheap shot at me. What goes around comes around was the mentality—or at least it was back then.

I remember going down for my pre-game nap and my mind would start racing. "Fuck, I wish I could just play right now and not think about what's going to happen." Knowing someone was going to drop the gloves. Someone was going to take a cheap shot.

But as soon as I got to the rink and was around the boys, nothing else mattered. The camaraderie in the dressing room, the joking around, the little things people don't see. It was my teammates who helped me stay relaxed, just by my being around them. And back then, players were relaxed because they knew their teammates were going to stick up for them no matter what. When I first got to the NHL, I knew for a fact that every time I was on the ice, there were two or three guys on our team who were willing combatants ready to stick up for me.

That changed. Towards the end of my career, I didn't know if my own teammates were going to back me up. There was a lot of uncertainty going into games. When everyone knew something was going to happen, they didn't want to be on the ice with you. You were kind of in no man's land by yourself. That's the way the game is now. Everyone is in it for themselves. You don't feel a sense of security with your own fucking teammates. You start to think, "Do I really want to hit this guy? I know I can fucking crush him. But who the fuck is going to jump in the pile with me?" Nobody.

I remember one night when I was playing for the Milwaukee Admirals during the 2004–05 NHL lockout. We played the Chicago Wolves pretty much every other weekend, and so naturally things got heated between the two teams.

In Chicago's old barn, both teams walked out to the ice through the same tunnel where the Zamboni came out. There was many a time when players would start yelling at each other in there. I remember one specific individual on the Wolves who started going off on me.

"You fucking low-life brown boy. Who the fuck do you think you are, coming into our barn and trying to run the show, you fucking greasy Indian?"

Our coach, Claude Noël, piped up for me, but those words hit me hard. I was thinking, "Fuck you, the way you talk to me. I'm going to get you in the next period." And the guy was a heavyweight.

Was I scared? Probably, because I knew that something was going to go down. But at the same time, all of my teammates heard the commotion, and with that group I knew they had my back. Put your workboots on, guys, it's going to be a fucking nasty period ahead. I looked them in the eyes and I could tell they were scared shitless. But they stood behind me that night.

I didn't always settle it with a fight. Most of the time when people started beaking me about being an Indian, I would just look at them and say, "Obviously you don't know who I am. I'm not a fucking Indian." It didn't affect me as much as it would have if I were an Indian person. I'm Inuk. Why would you think I'm Indian? That's when I started to realize that your average human being is not educated about the history of the First Nations people. We were all just labelled as Indians.

I didn't want to do anything like lodging a complaint with the team or the league. I was fine if everyone else talked about it, but not me. I didn't want the light shining on me because I was trying to break into the NHL and I didn't want it to affect my chances. It came down to fear of being exposed and fear of getting fucking cut. I didn't want anyone who was running the team thinking, "We don't want to deal with all this shit, so let's just cut Tootoo off the team."

I know there have been instances like that where teams cut a player because of the overwhelming pressure they were under as they tried to usher this First Nations athlete through the professional world. A lot of Indigenous athletes have been fucked over for political reasons. The teams and leagues already had enough shit going on, at least in their eyes. They're all part of the old boys' club, and they'd rather cover their backs than step out of line.

And now, finally, we're talking about it openly. I guess it was only a matter of time before leagues started to acknowledge what was happening. And it's not just hockey and it's not just the sporting world. It's happening in the corporate and business world as well.

For this to now come to light and people to be aware of it is a good thing. And it was a long time coming.

15 They Never Get Blown Over

I remember a moment of true happiness in my life.

I was probably twelve or thirteen years old. It was a Friday afternoon. My dad and Terence and I had packed up our quads to head out to Dad's cabin on Big Meliadine Lake, out by the mines outside of Rankin Inlet. Back then there were no roads. It was just a quad trail as soon as you left town.

My dad had these lookout points where we would stop and rest for a couple of minutes, because it's hard going on the rough terrain in the tundra. That day, I specifically remember that we walked up a hill. I looked over at my brother and my dad who were standing ten feet away from me. I remember my dad talking to Terence and my brother was sitting there, listening, idolizing this human being. Then my brother turned around and asked me, "Did you hear what Dad just said?"

"No," I said. "I wasn't close enough."

"He told me that this land is where we belong. This is where our people have survived. We can be resilient in surviving out here. I'm going to show you guys how."

I absorbed it all and said to myself, "This is where we belong." Whatever happened at home the night before doesn't matter here.

That's the moment when I connected my spirituality to our land. My thing is spirituality, not religion, and that's what I want to teach my kids.

The land is a healing mechanism for me, being able to reflect in nature. It brings me back to my childhood, watching my brother learning from my father. My dad passed down his teachings to my brother, and then my brother passed them down to me. I remember sleeping in a tent with my brother and thinking how great a life this is, away from society, away from the dysfunction.

My wife, Jen, is from an Italian family and was raised as a Christian. She wants to raise our kids in the church. But being in a church is not my thing and I'm not going to be forced into it. When I was a kid, my parents would drop us off at the church but never come in themselves. It was more babysitting—let's get rid of the kids for a few hours. My brother, my sister and I were the altar boys. I just went there because my buddies were there. I had no idea what was going on. I was forced and I was uncomfortable. There was no connection.

And now, with what we know about the church and residential schools, it's hard for me to pretend it wasn't their fault. How the fuck did they think that was okay? And you're preaching from the word of God?

I believe in God, but we all have our own way of believing. Aboriginal people have our own beliefs, and for me, it all comes back to the land.

My dad never really talked at home. But when he talked out on the land, you fucking listened. He's started coming out of his shell as I've gotten older, at least when he's in a place where he feels comfort, where he's safe, and he's able to express what he knows. Still, it's hard for him to articulate it through words. That's not the way he communicates.

We never had those teaching moments at home. It was on the land where he taught me.

When you're out there, everything is in the moment. And then, once that moment passes, it's out of his head. When you're out there, he might say, "The tide's low," or "It's really windy." My dad internalizes it without saying much.

He can spend hours and hours silently gazing. And then he'll spot a caribou across the bay.

"What the fuck are you talking about, Dad? Where?"

"You see that spot? You see that rock? Look in the scope."

And there it is . . .

You become accustomed to and aware of your surroundings through those kind of experiences, just letting your heart rate drop and focusing.

In all of our time on the land with my dad, I can't recall one incident that was life-threatening to us. Now, as an adult, I can protect myself, but I still don't feel safe out there without my dad. With him you have that extra layer of awareness. A lot of times we'd get caught up in what we were doing, like tying up the sled, but my dad would have a look around, take a few extra minutes to make sure there were no animals coming. There's always that predator that's out there that could fucking pop up out of nowhere. A lot of people in the south might think it's never going to happen to them. But safety first, that's my dad's motto.

My generation wants to get things done as quickly as possible—head down and not even be aware of what's around us. Dad's head's on a swivel all the time.

I'm fascinated and curious about him being so full of knowledge—and he doesn't even fucking know it. All self-taught, everything through actions.

I think about when I was a kid, ten or eleven years old, and how he went back to school in Medicine Hat to learn the plumber's trade. I realize it took a lot of courage and determination for him to open up a book again as a fucking forty-year-old. He hadn't done that since Grade 10. But he did it because he knew down inside that this was the best opportunity for him to provide for our family.

Throughout my years in adulthood, thinking back to those moments on the land has grounded me. It's been ingrained in me. It's where I find inner peace.

When I was drinking, I disrespected the land. Countless times I went out hungover to the gills. I'd be out in the wilderness, incoherent, and my dad was so patient and understanding. But I was being phony with myself.

And when I was a teenager coming home from playing junior hockey, I took advantage of the situation. One time I remember, we were going seal hunting the next morning and I fucking passed out in the canoe the night before because I didn't want to miss the trip. I had been out partying until 5 a.m. When I woke up, we were in the middle of Hudson Bay. I remember looking over at my dad and seeing the disappointment in his eyes because I had come out like that. I was lying to myself.

The first time I went out after I'd stopped drinking was very weird. I remember having this kind of out-of-body experience. I was thinking, "Do I really belong out here?" I knew how important it was to our people, but I also knew that I hadn't been practising the ways. It was very confusing, but in the end, the land grounded me.

My dad never drank when he was out on the land. He knew that all it takes is one mishap to get you killed out there. But his drinking can still be an issue. When I went home to visit, it was a great time for the two of us to go out for a couple of days. But it was always only a couple of days because my dad needed to get back to have his drink. It was that way even when we were kids—come Sunday, Dad would already be packing up because he was fucking getting the edge. "Oh, we're going home already? Why?" As kids, we didn't really understand. Now I know why.

When I go home as an adult I always tell him I want to go out for a week. He'll say he's game for it, but three, four days in, he's getting short-fused, he's getting irritated, because he's vibrating, thinking about getting his drinks.

———

When I left home at fourteen to play hockey, I lost many of the things that allow us to live and survive out there. I'm like a lot of our people who have lost their culture and heritage. I was in the southern life. I'd go home every summer, but slowly, gradually, I started to forget how to read the drifts of the snow—all the little random stuff—because I wasn't there every day anymore. I'd go home and all my buddies who I grew up with would turn it into a joke: "Oh, you're not an Inuk anymore, Jordin. You don't even know how to wrench on a quad."

Everyone has to know how to do their own shit out there. Now, I need somebody to help me because I've kind of lost that way of life. It's funny; my friends have some jealousy towards me because of playing hockey—"Oh, you can do whatever you want. You have so much money." Well, that's fine and dandy, but if you were in my shoes, you'd be thinking the other way— that they're the ones who are so lucky.

So when I go home now, a lot of my buddies are my teachers. I enjoy going out with them, but it's more of a watching thing for me. I could get by, but now I need their guidance.

For the Inuit people, the inukshuk has always represented our values and tradition. Growing up as a kid, we were taught how important they were, a way for our hunters to always know where they were.

And now I also think about them as a symbol of our resilience and mental toughness.

When I'm out on the land and I see an inukshuk, I think

to myself, "I wish I could be like one of them." That fucking thing can survive in anything—the harsh winters, the hot summers, the mosquitoes. They never get blown over. Imagine being naked and alone at minus-seventy, in a land where there is nothing to stop the wind. Somehow they survive—sometimes for hundreds of years.

And that's us.

Different nomad families had different designs for their inukshuks. It was a way to communicate with other groups. An inukshuk might mean that caribou herds come to that area, or muskox. If you're on a lake and you see one on top of a hill, you know that right down in front of it on the water is a good fishing spot. They carry all kinds of information. The inukshuk always faces north, so if snow piles up on the back of it, you know the wind is blowing to the north.

And they serve as markers in the terrain, especially in winter, when the tundra is white and flat and everything looks the same. Most of them are on top of ridges and hills, and usually, that part of the hill is bare land. If I were to ever get lost up in our wilderness, one of the first things that would go through my head would be to look for an inuksuk. Our people will build shelters just below them if they get lost.

Throughout my childhood, we'd go on winter hunting trips on the Ski-Doo, and then we'd go to the same spot in the summertime.

"Remember being here in February?" my dad would ask me.

"No. How do you know?"

"Well, see that inuksuk there? That's how I know."

It's funny. Living in the south now, I still couldn't tell you street names. For me, it's about looking at landmarks. Buildings, certain shapes and shit like that. That's how I navigate myself through big cities.

Although the inukshuk is not a living thing, it is for us. It's a sign of strength, resilience, protection, comfort, shelter.

When I see them down south in somebody's garden, it signifies nothing. It doesn't have any meaning. Do they actually know why they put it there? For show? It's just a decorative piece for their front lawn. Am I pissed off? No. Maybe in some small way it makes those people more aware of our people, and that's a good thing.

16 How Can a Person Have Both Good and Evil in Them?

I have told many difficult stories about my life and about my family, but this is the most difficult one I have ever told.

My uncle Luc was married to my auntie Dorothy, my dad's only sister, the only girl among ten kids in his family.

Luc and Dorothy started dating back in the eighties, when I was just a little kid. I always knew him as Uncle Luc, even before they got married. My brother, Terence, was the best man at their wedding, when he was only twelve years old.

Luc was from Quebec City. He was white, French Canadian. He worked for Air Canada for twenty-five years in the baggage handling department, loading and unloading the planes. My aunt Dorothy was a flight attendant for Air Canada for thirty years, so that's how they met. They didn't have any kids together, but my aunt Dorothy already had a daughter, and Luc became her stepfather.

Uncle Luc was a real working man, almost a workaholic. But it seemed to me that he also really enjoyed life. There was always a lot of laughter around him. And even though he came from outside of our family, he was the one who mended a lot of bridges in relationships. People seemed to naturally gravitate to Uncle Luc for advice, how to go about doing things a better way, and relied on him for his expertise in figuring shit out. He always seemed to have a logical solution to problems, so our family leaned on him for support and advice. He was a well-respected man who told it how it was.

When I was a young kid, we would see Uncle Luc and Aunt Dorothy when we went south for hockey schools, medical trips, holidays. We spent a week or two at their place in Winnipeg every summer. Uncle Luc was always a happy-go-lucky guy. I never ever suspected any hardships within him. He never showed that.

Later, they moved to Vancouver for work. I especially remember one trip there when I went out with my buddy Troy and his mom, Margo, so that Troy and I could attend the Wayne and Dave Babych Hockey School. I must have been eight or nine years old. We stayed at a hotel in the Vancouver suburbs, out near the arena where the hockey school was happening. That was my first real taste of a big city and Uncle Luc was the go-to guy. He brought us around—he seemed to always find time for family. Vancouver was a different world for me, and Uncle Luc was a breath of fresh air because you knew something unexpected was going to happen when you were with him—trips to the water park or golfing, stuff like that. I remember the stories we'd share and the laughs we had. It was almost like we didn't even need to talk about anything—we would just look at each other and there would be laughter, a good hard laugh about just senseless things. He had that aura around him. He was an outgoing guy who was always positive.

I feel like Uncle Luc knew what was going on at home with me and Terence because of the support he gave us. He knew our family dynamics. He was an outsider in that he wasn't a blood relative, but he knew my parents and what their issues were. He protected me and my brother by being truthful and honest. He took us under his wing. Uncle Luc brought us a lot of joy and helped us forget about all the painful interactions we had with our parents. It was almost the same way I feel when I'm out fishing or hunting and forget about the outside world for a while. That's the way I felt when I was with Uncle Luc. He was that kind of person.

When my brother, Terence, died in 2002, the whole family gathered in Brandon for his funeral. There were thirty or forty of us together in a conference room at the Keystone Centre before we headed over to the ceremony.

By that point, Uncle Luc had been sober for fifteen or twenty years. I actually have no memory of him drinking and I had never seen him drunk. I can only speculate as to why he'd quit drinking all those years before. I do know that most people have to hit rock bottom before they stop.

That day, I remember looking over at Uncle Luc and he was kind of pacing around the room, waiting for that moment to say something. When he finally spoke up, there was dead silence in the room and his voice was cracking. He said we had to clean up our act as a family. A few people stood up and agreed with him and said we needed to limit our intake of booze and whatever drugs people were taking. I remember listening to Uncle Luc and thinking, man, how come my dad couldn't do that? Why couldn't he say what Uncle Luc said? But looking back now, I realize my dad was struggling himself. Uncle Luc took the family leadership role, and I don't think there was a dry eye in that room that afternoon.

Uncle Luc was also important to my hockey career. He made a point of coming out and spending time with me wherever I was playing—junior, the minors, the NHL. He introduced me to my financial advisor and became my unofficial personal agent.

Early in my NHL career, he was constantly working the phones to get corporate deals for me in the North. People from home were always trying to pull me in different directions. I'd say, "Call my uncle Luc." That deterred a lot of them right away because they knew Uncle Luc was always looking out for my best interests. Any conversations that came up with friends or companies, he did all of the homework. A company would reach out to me and he'd say no, stay away from them—he always got the dirt on everyone.

My first year in the NHL, Uncle Luc reached out to one of the airlines that flies to Nunavut to see if I could do a couple of commercials for them in return for free tickets for my parents to come down to Winnipeg and see me. (It has always been very expensive to fly in the North.)

A competing airline, Canadian North, caught wind of that conversation. They were owned by Norterra, which ran a group of companies out of Edmonton. One of their big shots reached out to Uncle Luc and said they wanted to sign me to a three-year deal for six hundred grand to make appearances for them. When Uncle Luc came back to me with that I thought, "Holy shit, we're talking big money here for what I'm doing." I stayed with them for nine years.

I never, ever questioned Uncle Luc's decision-making on what was best for me. I trusted him. He did everything above and beyond my expectations without ever asking for anything for himself. I always felt bad about not being able to return the favours that he did for me. But he wouldn't take one frigging cent. I suspect he was conscious of my family dynamics and he knew that people living in the North seem to know everyone's business, so he didn't want anyone to think he was riding my coattails or using me for financial gain.

It was never like that. Any money that came in, he always made sure it was put straight into my investments. I trusted him without hesitating. No questions asked. He was one of the most important people in my life.

Uncle Luc was the first person I called when I went into rehab. He knew I had a drinking problem, but he had been letting me live my life. Every time he was in Nashville, he would go out with me, but I knew he would also get me home safe. I guess I kind of took it for granted. He was like a best friend who chaperoned me around. Wherever we went, it was always about what was best for Jordin, looking out for me so that I didn't get into any major shit. Whether it was at home or in Winnipeg or Nashville or whichever city I was in, Uncle Luc was there for me.

It's almost like he expected that I was going to wind up in rehab, or at least he was hoping it was going to happen sooner or later. When I called him and told him, it was like he knew I had a problem, but it wasn't like that stern, fight-back, telling me I should have gone in earlier. He just supported me. He wanted to give me space and let me live my life, but he was happy then that I was finally going to get help.

From the day I got out of rehab, Uncle Luc helped me change the way I thought about my finances. Now it was about planning for *my* family, the wife and kids I would have in the future. In the years past, I didn't give a shit about what I spent on whatever, whenever. Uncle Luc helped me change my mindset about enabling my parents by sending them money. One of the biggest things he said to me was that now that I was starting to have clarity, I had to start looking after myself and stop worrying about everyone else's financial problems. He protected me.

Uncle Luc and Aunt Dorothy moved up to Rankin Inlet after they left Vancouver. They both walked away from Air Canada on their own terms. My auntie always had projects on the go, even in retirement, and Uncle Luc was trained as a heavy equipment operator, so when he moved north he started working for one of the companies out at the mine. They lived in Rankin for a number of years and then eventually moved back to Winnipeg.

And that's the last place I saw my Uncle Luc.

In November 2020, I was in the city, doing a presentation. I remember texting Uncle Luc to tell him I was there. He was on his way in from Lac du Bonnet and picked me up at my hotel. We drove from downtown to his stepdaughter's house out by the airport for a visit.

I remember talking to Uncle Luc about life, about some issues he was having with his grandson, but nothing too heavy. Looking back, maybe Uncle Luc wasn't his usual loosey-goosey self. He was pacing and seemed a little tense, and he seemed relieved when I asked him to drive me back to the hotel. But on the drive we shared a few laughs like we always did. When he dropped me off, I told him to look after himself. And that was pretty much it.

I flew home to Kelowna the next morning. A day passed. And then the next afternoon, I got a call from Aunt Dorothy.

"Uncle Luc has passed away," she said.

What the fuck?

My first reaction was that he must have had a heart attack or something. Uncle Luc was a heavy smoker. He knew he had a problem. For fifteen or twenty years he said he was going to quit, but he never did. He'd had a couple of scares with his heart in the past. I thought that maybe he went to bed and just never woke up.

"No," Aunt Dorothy said. "He killed himself."

I was the first person she had called.

Hearing that instantly brought me back to the day my brother died. As soon as she said "suicide," my first reaction was "What the fuck is going on?" What's the story behind this? Why? Why would he do that? I was with him just two days ago.

A lot of people know how to hide when they're struggling, but I thought I was the one person that if he ever needed to say something or get something off his back, he would trust me with his secrets.

I was stone cold for the rest of the day. Jen was trying to comfort me. I was speechless. I kept thinking about how much he had done for me. I kept telling myself, "I'm going to be okay from here on in without Uncle Luc." I'm going to be okay because of the life lessons that he shared and how he helped me get through a lot of hard times.

But the last time I cried that much was when my brother passed away.

Aunt Dorothy asked me to speak at Uncle Luc's funeral. It was important to me to have the right words, so I wrote it out. I remember I made a note to myself on the first page to take a very big breath before I started, and then to look Uncle Luc's family straight in the eye.

It is breaking my heart to be here today. Auntie Dorothy, Tara, Brian, Brett, Tootoo Masha-May, Josee and Donavan.

I know how much you loved Taata and I know how much he loved you. You guys were his whole life, his everything. From Jen and I, our truest, deepest condolences. We feel your pain. And we are with you. We love you.

My name is Jordin, and Luc was my uncle. Uncle Luc was a truly beautiful man. There was never a dull moment. I mean, the guy could not sit still if you wanted him to. He was a go-getter. He was a man who had our backs. And, every one of us knew it. Every one of us has felt it at some point in our lives. We knew that if he was in our corner, we were safe.

Uncle Luc was a wise man. When I was a kid, breaking into the NHL, he's the guy who gave me the advice I needed. He always reminded me that I needed to be thinking about my future, and told me what steps I should take to make that happen. He taught me so many life lessons that I am so grateful for. He cared with a passion unlike anything I have ever seen.

He was an organizer. Sometimes to a fault. But we all truly embraced it as he always took control of any situation.

Uncle Luc was one of the most dedicated, hard-working men I've ever known. He gave it everything he had, full throttle all the way. I can guarantee every co-worker can attest to his charismatic personality and always looked forward to being around him, or else they were scared shitless of his brutal honesty.

Uncle was always down for an adventure. Everything from rock concerts to beach vacations. You know, he saved all of his concert tickets in a little box. Every single concert he's ever been to. He was an incredible man, he loved life. When he told stories he captivated a room.

He always talked about his next vacation. He loved the heat, but more importantly the water.

Some of my best memories are of us out on the land. I remember one time we were camping, I was relaxing in the tent, and all I could hear was him howling. I mean, he couldn't stop. I was just drinking my tea and I started to get the giggles, knowing that whatever it was . . . it was really good. And so he poked his head into the tent and told me to come out. And we all know when he is laughing so hard, how red his face gets and his veins are popping out. After showing me what he did, he and I literally could not stop laughing for what must have been half an hour straight. I'll have to keep that part of the story between him and me.

I want you all to pause and reflect on a personal moment you had with Uncle Luc and relive the laughter you had with him . . .

Uncle, you touched so many lives and I want to acknowledge everyone here. May we all use his infectious energy and laughter to live life to the fullest and continue to create life-long memories with one another.

And, like many of us, Uncle Luc fought demons inside his own mind, which none of us knew about. I hope that maybe a small bit of good can come from his passing. And that is that we use this as an opportunity to talk to one another about how we really feel. Especially we as men need to let our guards and pride down. To know that being vulnerable is okay. Every one of us fights a fight nobody knows about, and if we open those communication lines to one another, together, we can break this cycle.

My final words to you, Uncle: you will forever hold a place in my heart.

But I feel comfort and peace knowing that you and Terence are reunited.

I love you, may you rest in peace,

Lukasii niek.

After the funeral, the conversations continued, and so did the digging. I was in contact with Aunt Dorothy for weeks. There was a lot of mourning. Everyone was in shock. And at that time, no one knew the whole story. I don't think Aunt Dorothy even knew. There were things she was finding in and around the house that led to a lot of suspicions as to why he had done what he did.

And then she found the letter that he sent her.

A lot of unexpected deaths bring out the cold, hard truth about the lives lived.

In writing my books, I have always tried to be as honest as possible. But in this case, I am not going to be able to do that, because it would hurt other, innocent people.

My experiences with Uncle Luc while he was alive were nothing but positive. Until the day he passed, I'd never had a blow-up with him. There was no animosity We had lots of conversations about life. When there were hardships in the family, we'd talk about them, but we always ended up in a laugh—right up until fucking two days before he died. But obviously, looking back, there was a lot he didn't tell me. He never talked about his life growing up or his experiences as a teenager or when he was using alcohol. It was always focused on me, and my challenges, on how he could help Jordin.

It never crossed my mind that he was struggling mentally—ever. I had never suspected he was damaged inside. The guy lit up a room and got shit done. People wanted to be around him because he was a person to lean on for anything.

My stomach gets knotted up thinking about him. But I could only go on what I experienced. It's just so frustrating, finding out the dark side of people you think you're close to.

But now, knowing what I know—and I hate knowing what I know—if he was still around, there's no possible way I'd be able to hold myself back from laying a beatdown on him.

How do I explain in my own words those two different people? Fifty per cent of your mind and body tells you that you love that person for everything he did for you. And the other half tells you, "Fuck this person for what he did to someone else." He was only good for me and I loved the guy, and at the same time someone else wished he was dead. I can't go back to loving him the way I did before knowing what he did. How do you look at him the same way?

And did I miss something?

I still talk with people back home who knew Uncle Luc, and they talk about how much he did for me and what a tragedy it is that he's gone. I have to hold my tongue a lot. I guarantee you that if he were still alive, there is no way he would be able to see me face to face. No fucking way. My brain tells me that I would fucking kill this guy—and I'd have no remorse.

My dad and Uncle Luc are two different people on two different ends of the spectrum. But it's that same question about how a person can have both good and evil in them. How do I find the words that explain that character?

In speaking with a few people who have experienced verbal and physical abuse, the idea that stuck out to me is that the ones you are closest to are the ones who are most likely to be doing evil to you because of the trust factor.

It amazes me how many people my dad has fooled over the years. When newcomers come to town, when my buddies come to town, when my friends are around, he can be an amazing person. Everyone loves Barney Tootoo because he's so charismatic, he's so gentle, he's so thoughtful and soft-spoken. This is the face that he puts out to the public. I think, "Why the fuck is he not like this all the time?" He saves the fucking nastiness for his own family.

My dad would come down to Nashville when I was playing there and go on his weekend benders. I'd buy him a one-way ticket just to get him away from my mom for a little while and give her a break. He figured it out pretty darned quick. He would sit in the corner of the bar and quietly drink his face off. Sometimes he would drag one of my buddies along with him and keep them up until four in the morning, even though they wanted to go home—and that pushed some of them away from him. But he was a happy drunk there. None of the anger, none of the violence. Why couldn't he be like that at home?

The people who met him in situations like that, or when they were visiting Rankin, wouldn't recognize the Dad I grew up with, at least the one behind closed doors.

I remember when I was nine or ten years old, Mom pulling us out of bed in the middle of the night, going to the airport and jumping on the first fucking flight to get out of town to get away from him. We would fly to Churchill or Baker Lake—wherever my grandmother was living at the time. But we always came back in a couple of days.

Even in early adulthood, I was fucking terrified of him. But then we would be out on the land. For him, it was cleansing. He could wash everything out. Out on the land, you're not being seen by anybody in town. You don't have to wrestle with the thoughts of what you did the night before. The damage that he'd done was erased because this amazing, wise, patient man was showing me how to cut up a caribou.

What is the thought process for him out there? When we were out on the land after two days of him being on a fucking bender, was he trying to process everything that had happened and then trying to make it right for his kids by being the best dad? Every time he did something amazing for my family, it washed away everything that happened in the latest episode. I was built to be pretty quick to forget about what happened. Maybe that's why he did it.

But that's the guy I wish was my everyday Dad. In my dreams, I wish we just lived out on the land, even though I know that the reality is it would be a gong show because he would start having his booze cravings after three or four days.

Nobody would have these issues if they lived like his parents did, if we were all still fucking nomads, the way it used to be. We would be living a hard life, but a good life. Everything changed when they moved to town to find work and suddenly the booze was never-ending. It sometimes feels like everyone up there is a functional substance abuser in some sort of fashion. My father's generation had zero experience articulating their feelings and putting them into words. They use substances to mask their feelings and become somebody they don't really want to be. Part of me feels sad for my dad because he was never taught how to communicate and verbalize.

If I was still using, if I was still addicted to alcohol, all of this would eat me up inside. I would use and it would create more issues. If I was still drinking, I would think about Dad and Uncle Luc and I would drink to fucking hate them and hopefully cross paths with and beat the shit out of them. Today I am able to talk about it and not get overly ramped up and not revert to substances to help me numb the pain. Today I am sober and I am okay with not knowing all the answers. I'm doing everything in my power to process it. I'm not allowing past experiences to drag me back down the rabbit hole and back to having dark thoughts.

Whether you have resentment or hatred, it's up to you to be able to let go of it.

I will never know what drove Uncle Luc to do what he did, and I've come to terms over the last year and a half with the fact I may never know why my dad is the way he is. I may not know until he's on his deathbed—and even then he may not say anything. I have learned to move on and move past situations that have harmed a lot of people, including me.

I'm not closing the doors yet. That door is always going to be open. I may never know the answers. But that may have to be the way it is.

17　I Don't Ever Count My People Out

Normally, I make a yearly trip home to Rankin Inlet. It's a big part of my process of cleansing my mind and body, to get up there and get out on the land. After I was vaccinated, I finally had the chance to go back in the summer of 2021. It's the perfect time of year to be there. The hunting is great. The fishing is great.

But this time, I had another reason to go: the chance to try and get my father to talk about his experience in the residential school.

It had been almost two years, but it felt like it had been ten years since I'd gone home. I was a little nervous as to how my family was going to react. But when I landed there and I got my two feet on the ground in Nunavut, it was an emotional release. I was home.

I went up with a clear mindset. No worries. I wasn't stressing over when the next episode with my parents was going to happen. On prior trips, that was constantly on my mind.

I was by myself, so I didn't have to worry about Jen and the girls if I was out on the land for hours. I was able to pick up and go whenever I wanted, which was kind of nice because everything's spontaneous up there. The weather changes all the time. One day it's clear and sunny, let's go on Hudson Bay. Next day it's windy, let's go up to Big Meliadine Lake instead.

When I arrived, a lot of tears were shed. There's FaceTime and all that, but being in each other's presence for real was humbling. When I got to my parents' home, I just sat on the couch. It was kind of funny—there was a lot of silence. It's almost like we didn't know how to talk with each other because we hadn't been around each other for so long. But it was just nice to be in each other's presence. I was there, my parents were there, and I felt a sense of security.

We had about thirty minutes of just me, my mom and my dad before the revolving door started and people started piling in. But in those thirty minutes I could see it in my mom's eyes: the feeling of relief because I had finally made it home. She didn't say it, but I could tell she was thinking, "I'm in safe hands with Jordin around." I don't think I've ever hugged my mom for that long and that tight.

And my dad had the biggest smile on his face. He asked me, "Where do you want to go? What do you want to do? What do you want to hunt?" He went out to his garage and started futzing around, getting stuff ready in case the weather turned, in anticipation of getting out on the land. I could see he had an itch to get out.

My dad was in good shape the whole trip. I was going to bed every night at nine or nine thirty and I'd wake up around seven the next morning, and if my dad was still sleeping, I figured he might have snuck to the garage for a few nightcaps. But it wasn't like he was sitting in the living room drinking beer. I knew he went out a few nights next door to his buddy's place after I'd gone to bed, but there was none of the usual yelling and screaming when he'd come home.

The next day, right around dinnertime, I said to my dad, "Hey, it's Monday tomorrow, everyone's cool. Maybe we should go out to Big Meliadine for the day—just you and me." And *boom*, within ten minutes of me asking him, he was in the garage, getting his quad ready. You could see the excitement through his actions.

My dad is not a very vocal or animated person. But I know what makes him happy. If I say, "Dad, where are all your five-gallon jerry cans? Let's go fill them up," he'll say, "Oh, you don't have to do that, Jordin. I can do it myself. Don't worry."

But the smile on his face tells me how he feels, knowing that he'll have enough fuel to go whenever and wherever he wants.

Monday morning, we headed out, and stayed out for at least twelve hours. I felt like I was really engaged in listening to my dad. He's getting a little older, but still doing the things that he wants. I wanted it to be in a peaceful setting where, whatever help my dad needed, I was right there for him.

When we were on the lake in our boat, I felt like I was a little kid again. I would be tying the hook onto the line and other stuff like that, and he'd say, "No, I'll do that for you, Jordin."

I wouldn't argue. If he wanted to do it, I would just let him do it because I wanted him to feel safe and in a good space.

At the end of our day fishing, we went to my dad's little square box cabin at the north end of the lake. We stopped and beached the boat and sat down to have a tea and some lunch on the shore of the lake. I thought that was the time to try and get him to answer all of the questions I had.

"Dad, you know I love you and I'm grateful for everything that you've taught me, and still to this day showing me the way of life up here. And I want to keep learning because I feel like, since I've been gone for twenty-five years, I've lost a lot of those little things. When you're around it every day, it seems natural. But for me now, it's almost like I'm a young kid, learning all over again just by watching you . . ."

He was nodding his head.

I started talking about myself and what I had experienced. I didn't mention any of the bad episodes with him. I just wanted to praise him for everything that he's taught me.

"Dad, you know my life story. But not a lot of people know how you grew up and where you grew up. I know very little. You grew up in Churchill, but where were the other parts of your life?"

"Well, as a young kid we were kind of nomads," he said. "We hunted for our food and eventually we all moved to Churchill. But I don't really remember my early years."

"What do you mean?" I asked him.

"I just can't remember."

I kept trying to navigate through, trying to get him to reflect, but I didn't want to push the wrong button because I didn't want the moment to be ruined.

It went silent there for a few minutes while I gazed out at the land and waited for him to keep talking. But as soon as he shut down and said, "I don't remember," I thought, "Fuck, he does, but he doesn't want to say."

I halted the conversation there because I could feel him thinking, "Where are you trying to go with this, Jordin?" It's hard for me to find the words to make him feel safe. But I thought that maybe just being out there on the land would be his security blanket.

It's almost like I had it on the tip of my tongue. I didn't want to start getting frustrated or angry about not being able to get info out of him. I remember at one point out in the boat, I was thinking to myself, "Should I just ask him, like, what the fuck happened? What's our family secret?" But then it was like, "Fuck, I can't." Instead I got up and threw a line in the water to let my mind and body cool down. Hopefully catch a fish and let that conversation pass through my dad's head. But that was it. Nothing more was said, and eventually we went home.

It's funny—afterwards, it was like the conversation between us out there never even existed.

A few days went by, and we went back to Big Meliadine, but this time we had to bring out scientists who were testing the waters for contamination from the mine that is nearby. There was no fucking way I was going to be able to try and talk with my dad with them around.

It's crazy how the little kid in me comes out every time there's a situation within my family. That little scared boy comes out, telling me, "Don't ask Dad in front of all these people. He's going to get a fucking lip on, and then the scientists are going to wonder what the hell's going on. Why is he all pissed off and short and quiet? Usually he's pretty vocal and bubbly and loves to talk with people like that."

We were out with them for hours and I was just kind of a spectator. I kept fishing while the scientists did all of their water testing and Dad piloted the boat.

My dad's not very vocal, but when he talks about an experience out on the land or the weather patterns, he opens up.

"The wind's coming from the south," he said. "It's going to get fucking nasty. We should probably head back soon."

I was thinking, "Fuck, why do we have to go back already, Dad?" I was thinking that he wanted to get back home to have his drinks. I had seen it so many times before.

But by the time we got back to the cabin, it really was fucking windy as hell and the water was getting pretty choppy. He was right about the weather. I realized that my dad's getting older. He's not a young whippersnapper anymore and can't drive the boat and make sure everyone's okay like he used to.

We dropped off the quads, and then we headed home.

After that fishing trip, a couple of days went by. There was a lot of just hanging around the house. I asked my dad, "What's the daily routine here? You get up, have your coffee, go for a drive around nine o'clock. That's it?" After a few days of doing that, I was kind of mentally drained because everyone around town wanted to see me. And I'm a person who loves "me time," just being alone and being in my own thoughts. I was only going to be in Rankin for a short amount of time. I didn't want to just go for a drive and have to talk to everybody and by mid-afternoon be fucking drained from socializing.

So, anytime my parents would go out, it was quiet time for me at home.

My mom would always say, "Are you going to be okay if you're alone?"

"Yeah, Mom," I told her. "I'm old enough to look after myself now."

My mom's always been that way . . .

But there was another reason I didn't want to go on those drives around town. In the years past, I felt like I was taken advantage of. Every time my parents wanted to go out for a drive, they would head for the store and walk the aisles. They were thinking, "If we've got Jordin with us, he'll slap his credit card down and buy us whatever we want."

I enabled that.

And now, in sobriety and looking at my life, I take these opportunities to set boundaries and say no. I'm not going for a ride. I'm just going to stay home. When I told my parents that, you could see the tension in their body language—as though they were thinking, "Well, frick . . ."

———

One of the highlights of my trip home came a few days later, when we got out on Hudson Bay and went whale hunting. My brother-in-law has a big boat for open water. I told my sister the night before that I didn't want her inviting all of her friends onto the boat. "Can it just be me, you, your husband and your four kids? Let's just have only-us time."

That's what she did, and it was fucking awesome. It was just the seven of us, being in each other's presence without anybody around. I had never really had that experience with my sister and her whole family before, because there's so many people around constantly.

We were chasing a beluga whale, and my niece Jayda came up to me—she's twenty years old now—and said, "We're going to play rock-paper-scissors to see who goes after the first whale."

"Jayda, I haven't been home in two years," I said. "Are you serious? You're not going to let Uncle go first?"

"No," she said.

So, we played rock-paper-scissors, and of course she won, so she got to carry the harpoon first.

This is old-school hunting. It's an adrenalin rush. When you're at the front of the boat, holding the harpoon, chasing the beluga whale, it's like fucking lightning goes through you. The spotlight's on you. It's almost like when I played hockey. Everyone's fucking watching you. All the other hunters are telling you how to navigate, when to throw the harpoon. Those are the little things I don't know anymore. When you're not around it every day or doing the things that our people do, you lose a lot of those subtle skills that are required. I've got my sixteen-year-old nephew telling me when to throw the harpoon and I'm thinking, "Fuck, these are the things I wish I knew."

Jayda harpooned the whale, and then we shot it to finish it off. After that we tied a rope around the tail and dragged it to shore. It usually takes four or five people to drag it up the shoreline as far as possible. You have to know whether the tide is coming in or going out. You need a couple of bear watchers constantly looking around for any bears to pop up. It's a race against time to cut it all up and get back in the boat and to safety. We take the white skin and a little bit of fat off the whale—it's called *muktuk* and it's delicious. Once we've done that, we tie the carcass to the boat and drag it forty or fifty yards offshore and let it sink to the bottom, to return it to where it belongs. It is picked clean by other sea creatures within hours.

During my time in Rankin, I had a couple of evenings when I got to visit some of my friends—especially Pujjuut Kusugak. I spent as much time hanging out with Pujjuut as I could. I love that guy. He's just so educated in our traditions and culture and history.

We got to talking about residential schools. I really wanted to talk to him about my dad.

His dad's family and my dad's family kind of grew up together. Pujjuut's family all experienced residential schools.

"There's a lot of fucking trauma that our family has endured, but no one's fucking talking," he told me. "At least you still have your dad around."

Pujjuut's dad passed away years ago. "Growing up," he said, "I envied you and your brother because your dad always took you guys out on the land." His dad was a politician, and he was gone all the time and didn't spend a lot of time out on the land.

I asked Pujjuut if he had any ideas about getting my dad to talk about his residential school experience. He knows how my dad is. His thought was that if I talked to my dad about mental toughness—if I asked him how he became mentally strong—that might be a place to start. I obviously got my mental toughness from somewhere, and I believe a lot of it's from my dad. He taught me how to overcome. But we never, ever talked about it. It's hard to engage in a deep conversation with my dad. He doesn't dive into his feelings. He's never had to go there.

I talked to Pujjuut about the connections between our families. We had never, ever had those conversations before, where it was just me and him. Never. There were always other people around. Pujjuut's gone through a lot himself, and he's one of the guys in our community who people tend to lean on. Being around and listening to him speak really gave me a better understanding of how not only our family but also our entire community has been affected and what it's led to—all the fucking trauma.

Pujjuut is battling his own demons in sobriety, and he needed me to help him get through those battles. I'm forever grateful that I'm able to do that for him. He told me he was ready to pick up and start drinking again. Well, fuck, how do you say no?

Our conversation just kind of took off. We started talking about people we knew who are our uncles' ages, in their fifties and sixties. He had heard stories about their experiences in residential schools. Pujjuut's been sober now for two years, and it's only now that he is really starting to realize the effects of residential schools, the intergenerational trauma that's been passed down.

I was in Rankin for ten days. There were three fricking suicides during that time—two in my community and one in another community nearby.

"It's so fucking crazy how it's normalized," Pujjuut said. "When people are down, they revert to the threat of 'Well, fuck, I might as well just kill myself. I'm a failure.' It's fucked up, how it's an open conversation. People have young kids running around their house and they're saying, 'Well, fuck, I might as well just kill myself. It's better if I'm not here.' You talk like that in front of your kids, no wonder it becomes the norm for them by the time they're fucking ten, eleven, twelve years old. No wonder they think that suicide is almost okay."

Two of the three individuals who took their lives when I was home that summer were guys Terence went to school with.

The Tootoo family was always looked upon as a family of wealth and structure and success in Rankin Inlet. Now I look back and remember all the shit I had to deal with—and people thought our life was great. Then I look at those people who took their lives and look at their family dynamics, and I guarantee they lived twice as hard as we did.

You don't know what's going on behind closed doors in

remote communities and on reserves. I actually see it more today, when I am on public speaking trips, than I did when I was growing up in Rankin. I visit households, and when I walk through those doors, everyone seems happy. But there's an aura. Everything is worn down. There's the stagnant air. There's shit everywhere. There are holes in the walls—and every damn hole tells a story about substance abuse or mental health issues or physical and verbal abuse. If only those walls could talk. Man, as parents, how can you allow this filth in your house? A lot of these people have accepted that this is their life.

I was actually pretty fucking fortunate to grow up in a home where my parents kept our house in order. There wasn't shit everywhere. My parents put on a show for people who came into our home—that's why people thought we were so lucky, that we were the family that had everything. And the real shit that was going on in my house went unnoticed.

So many of the people taking their own lives are in their mid-forties and early fifties—the kids of the seventies and eighties. It has to be because of all the generational trauma that was passed down. The only question is not if, but when the next person is going to kill themselves. How do you break that cycle?

I've heard it from my sister, fucking talking about killing herself in front of her kids. She's forty-four years old. Her kids are all teenagers. And you're fucking saying you're about to do yourself in and that life will be better without you? It's okay to talk like that after losing a sibling? My mom has even talked about suicide when my dad's on a rampage.

I've got my nephews and nieces seeing the shit going on. It's just psychologically wrong. It's that constant threat: "I'm the victim. Poor me. You guys did this to me." You see that in a lot of Indigenous communities. Blaming everyone else.

But it's hard for me to tell myself that our people weren't fucked over by the government and fucked over by the church. How the fuck did they think that was okay?

Our people always say, "Let's let time pass, everything will be okay." We've been saying that for years. Our people don't want to face the issue head-on. They'd much rather say, "Sleep it off. It'll be okay in a few days."

You've got to look at their fucking history. But that's me being able to see the other side, how they were put in a situation that ultimately made them want to take their own lives.

When you live in a remote community, all you need to know is what you need to do to survive that day. Our grandparents lived in a different generation. They only knew what they knew. They were limited as to their education, and then their culture and beliefs were taken away from them. They mean everything to us because they teach us our traditions, but I understand how hard it must be for them to let go and let their grandkids explore the world after all the damage that was done to them.

I wouldn't have understood that if I hadn't left the North. I don't consider myself better than anyone else—especially my people—just because I had the chance to move down south. I get that a lot from community members—"You think you're better than us and now you come back and try to change everything."

I left home when I was fourteen years old. I moved to better educate myself and to see how much more was out there. And now, by living down south, I can give my own kids an opportunity to see the world and not to be closed-minded.

For many years, especially in my early twenties, I really did think I was going to go back home and change the world. I realized how much of an impact I could make on our people just by being present, and I started to think that maybe I would be the one to—not change our way of life, but bring a healthier way of living into our homes.

It took me a long time to realize that it takes a team. It takes everybody to make change happen. You need support. But I also understand that the idea of allowing settlers to help us to be successful is not acceptable among a lot of our people because of the damage done.

Don't get me wrong—I don't ever count my people out. We are resilient. We just need to stand for ourselves and show people the strength and mental toughness that is already there. Instead, we seem to always revert to blaming somebody else because of history.

So, what can I do to change the mindset of our youth? The guys who killed themselves while I was in Rankin all had kids who are teenagers. Now those kids will be struggling for the rest of their lives, and they might say, "Well, life's too hard and I'll just do what Dad did."

I think we need to start sharing our experiences with other people. We need to become connected on a deeper mental level. We've never been there before. It's all new to us.

It's about hearing us out. We want to be fucking heard. Just be supportive. Don't tell me what I need to do for the next steps.

But on the flip side, a lot of our people want change tomorrow. Well, fuck, it takes time. You've got to let the process happen. I hate getting into political shit, but when a political party says they're going to do something and it doesn't happen for a couple of years, our communities are back to where we used to be in the past, where you don't trust the white man because they're fucking lying to us again. They tell us what we want to hear, but they don't follow through.

I'm trying to mend those relationships by going out and allowing people to hear me talk about letting outsiders in in order for us to move forward. We need help. We always say we're going to do it on our own, but nothing's fucking happening.

Nobody wants to take the bull by the horns because so many of us are fighting inner demons ourselves. I see the trap that we're in. But in order to expand our thoughts and our learning, we've got to get outside the box and look from the outside in. When you're inside this cloud, you're surviving here, but you don't realize that the substance abuse, the domestic abuse—as I've said before, all that shit is not normal. It's not. What happens when a kid leaves one of our communities to get an education? A lot of them want to come home. That's fine. Culture shock is natural. But getting homesick for addiction or violence? A lot of things are better back home. But we need to be honest with ourselves about the things that aren't.

And some of our own leaders have let us down. I've sat in many boardrooms on the reserves and been just fucking livid because of what I've heard. Councillors making decisions for their own benefit, not for the benefit of their people.

Meanwhile, your average white Canadian is saying, "Why can't you get your shit together? I did it—and I did it on my own. Why can't you people fucking do it?" Well, yeah—in the white man's world. What they're really saying is "Fucking drunk Indian—if I can do it, why can't he do it?"

Have you ever experienced intergenerational trauma? It's easy to say, but it's another to walk the walk.

The last day before I left Rankin, my dad and I went out on the land with Hunter Tootoo, who is Dad's nephew—Hunter's father was my dad's oldest brother. Hunter is another person whose mind I would love to fucking dive into, because he experienced residential school. He lost his career as a politician because of drinking, he went to rehab. I just hope he's not back drinking again. I asked my auntie Dorothy, "What's the fucking deal with Hunter? He's not back on the sauce, is he? What's going on?" I've seen it before. Something happens, and you go back to your old ways.

But she wasn't going to say nothing. What's with all the family secrets? No one's fucking talking. It's not like I'm going to go and fucking advertise it to the world during my next interview. I don't know what the fear is. I just don't understand it.

Hunter's father was a major alcoholic. He literally had a fucking bottle of beer in his hand on his deathbed. I wish I could understand what happened to them.

That day, out on the boat, there were zero fucking conversations about life. Hunter and my dad were sharing old stories about the happy times. There's never any stories about the tough, hard times.

I tried talking to Hunter about what he'd been going through, but it was all surface stuff—"I got this new job, I'm grinding away, blah, blah, blah."

"But how are you *doing*?"

"Oh, I'm good."

No, you're not fucking good. But I'm not going to tell you because I'm not here to judge and say you need to fucking stay sober. That's not my place. Although I would love to say, "Look, I know you're a grown-up man now and I can't tell you what to do. But here's what I've experienced."

It's unfortunate. He's a very educated man with a lot of experience under his belt. Fuck, let it out, man. But it's easy for me to say that, right?

18 I'm Going to Keep Taking a Run at This for as Long as It Takes Me

My flight home was at four in the afternoon. When I got up for the day, all the kids had gone to school, and it was just me, my mom and my dad.

I think for the first time in my life, I didn't hear my mom say, "Well, you're already leaving us. I haven't seen you at all." On my prior trips I was always going here, visiting this person, being pulled to this school, which was totally fine by me because it helped me get through those long days at home. But I felt that on this trip we spent a lot of quality time together. I could really see it in the happiness around the house and the calm. No fucking drama other than the daily yelling and bossing around the people who come in the house. But other than that, it was actually refreshing for me. It wasn't so stressful.

That last day, we drove around town. It was just the three of us the whole morning.

I really wanted to ask questions. But I didn't want to leave on a sour note. I felt defeated. I didn't accomplish my goal, and throughout my life every goal that I have set for myself I have always accomplished. It put me in my place. I thought I was going to be able to get through to my dad and get those answers.

But now I look at it as another hurdle that I need to overcome. I need to educate myself more. I need to do my part. I need to see a therapist who specializes in PTSD—someone who has experience with people who went to residential schools. My goal right now is to have a bunch of sessions with that individual and educate myself on how to approach my dad and have a better understanding of PTSD. And then take another run at it.

I'm going to keep taking a run at this for as long as it takes me.

I owe that to my dad.

The day I beat the shit out of my father, I was nineteen years old. It was the summer before my last season of junior hockey in Brandon, and I was home in Rankin Inlet.

It was midday. My mother and father and sister and I were sitting in the house. We were still half-cut from drinking the night before and were sitting on our couch having a few more drinks. I could feel the shift happening with my dad, where he turns angry and mean. He started directing comments towards my mom over something stupid, and I thought "Here we go. It's two o'clock in the afternoon and this shit has already started."

When you're hungover, you're easily agitated. Your filters are fucking high. Your stress levels are tapped out because of anxiety.

That day I could feel the tension rising. As the hours went by, I started becoming verbally abusive towards my dad, trying to stand up for my mom. The conversation heated up. That was the first time my father had ever encountered push-back from the ones closest to him. And he didn't like it.

Then I fucking snapped. I felt like it was my opportunity to make a stand. I wrestled with a lot of fear in that moment. But a person can only handle so much before they explode. That's human nature and it's intensified when you have substances in your body. You're looking for something else to blame other than the substances that are altering your mind.

I blacked out. The next thing I knew, the house was upside down.

What the fuck did I do?

You block out certain memories in your life. I blocked out that episode until I started writing my first book. That's when the memories started coming back and I relived those moments and those emotions with the help of talking to my mom and my sister about what went down.

It was a turning point. There was a shift regarding the way my dad behaved towards my mom, at least when I was around. After that fight he had to watch what he said and how he acted because he knew his son wasn't scared of him anymore.

You can't turn back time. Whatever happened happened.

But I feel bad about that day. How could I do something like that to an already broken person? When I look back, knowing what I know now, I have a lot of guilt.

I think of how proud I was in that moment. I handed my sister my dad's ripped, bloody T-shirt like it was a trophy. I feel bad for letting Dad know who was boss. That wasn't a moment to be proud of. But how are you supposed to sympathize with someone who did the shit that he did? It was tough to swallow, not just that day but also all the years before and after.

Now I understand that's not who my dad really is. When you have a little sympathy, it allows you to look beyond those moments and look beyond the history. What I have learned about my dad's life and what he experienced has changed the way I feel about him. I think I have a better understanding now of how my dad processes hard times. He's an intelligent man who is scarred.

I don't resent my parents for their actions anymore. I don't put all the blame on them. As adults, we all know right from wrong. But there are things that we do that we don't quite understand ourselves until we face ourselves in the mirror—as hard as it may be. To move forward, you have to let those emotions sit in your gut.

I'm learning. I'm going through the process of absorbing my life and my experiences and using that to be a better person. That's how you grow. That's how you create character.

I look back and think about the what-ifs.

What if my dad hadn't been the person he was? What if he'd been sober? Would I be who I am today?

Would I be the person I am today if there'd been no drama in my house? Probably not. I probably wouldn't even be a hockey player. Sports were an outlet for me. I played all sports because I wanted to be at the gym, at the arena, at the soccer field and get away from being trapped in those four walls. Hockey was my escape. But I didn't really understand that as a kid. I did what felt like fun.

And there was no fun at home.

My upbringing created this fire inside me and has given me purpose in life. If I had the choice, I would still want to have the experiences that I had, because it has allowed me to take those leaps and explore the unknowns and not worry about what the future might hold. It's allowed me to live life for today.

Having negative experiences builds character, and that's the same for everyone, in all walks of life. I know there are non-Indigenous people who understand what I'm talking about. Everybody has gone through it whether they are wealthy or poor or white or Aboriginal—it doesn't discriminate. I don't care if you're the happiest person in the world—there is probably a lot of shit that you've gone through to get to that point. You know what *mind over matter* means, even if you haven't ever thought of it that way.

I have done a lot of self-reflection, and I have had to take a lot of deep breaths. I understand now that we all have emotions, and we need to let them out. I'm not afraid to shed a tear in front of people even though I have the image of being this tough, hard-nosed guy. It took me a long time to understand what vulnerability means.

I wish the people I love and who are closest to me would be able to see what I see now, today. I went through experiences that no one should ever go through. Some of them were my own fault.

But they made me who I am.

I have dreams about my brother, dreams about us being together. They started right after he passed.

We are out on the bay and my brother is on the boat. I'm on land. And he says, "Okay Jor, I've got to go check the nets." And he just drifts off, and *boom*, I wake up. It would kind of freak me out in the moment.

Other times, we are on quads out on the land. "Okay Jordin," he says. "You go down this trail, I go down this trail, and we'll meet at the end." Then I wake up and think, "What the fuck?"

Or we are jumping out of an airplane together, skydiving, and we go our separate ways.

The common theme is: "Jordin, you're going to be okay. Go on your own. I'm going to go this way."

When I first started having those dreams, I felt disturbed. But then they started to give me a lot of peace, knowing that his spirit is still with me.

I feel him the most when I am holding a rod, in a tree stand, fishing or hunting, visualizing him there with me.

It brings me back to the land. And that's where we become powerful.

Acknowledgments

I need to start with thanks to my parents. You have given me the strength to be the man I am today.

I have been blessed to work with Stephen Brunt on this book. Thank you, Stephen. You have an amazing ability to capture my voice. I don't know how you do it. It is a special gift.

There are some incredible people who helped shape my life. You were the ones who saw something more in me and encouraged me to be better. You know who you are. Thank you.

Mike Watson. You, my friend, have sparked the fire under me to know what my true purpose is in life. To give back to our Indigenous communities. We have shared the same journey in sobriety and I'm truly grateful for your leadership and insights.

To my dear brother Terence, I would not have had the success I had without you by my side for the first nineteen years of my life and without your teaching. You are my hero, bro.

My first book was dedicated to the memory of my brother, Terence. Terence, I still feel you by my side. When I'm out on the land I can hear your voice. Thank you for all you did to set me on the right path.

Most importantly, I want to thank my wife, Jen, and our daughters, Siena and Avery. You are my world. You give my life meaning. You are my hope for the future.

Index